"Digital isn't just another channel, it's the enabler for the next generation of buying experiences, which are asynchronous and buyer driven. Bill Stinnett lays out a wonderful road map of how to be successful in this age. This book is invaluable for any seller!"

Amir Jafri, Worldwide Sales CTO, Cross Solutions
Microsoft

"Stinnett's approach to collecting and curating the digital selling content that many companies already have is terrific! This book will show you how to build a powerful arsenal of assets that your sales teams can use to create and close new sales opportunities. Lots of actionable, detailed advice on leveraging and executing your social strategy. I've enjoyed it immensely!"

Stephanie Nashawaty, SVP and Chief Customer Innovation Officer
SAP

"I found *The Digital Selling Handbook* both interesting and immediately applicable to anyone with the privilege to touch the sales function in any way. This book demystifies digital. If you are involved in any aspect of the commercial motion, you will read this and have clear things you can immediately do to drive better results!"

Maria Boulden, Vice President, Executive Partner, Sales
Gartner

"Let me start by saying I loved this book! I literally couldn't put it down. I'm 100% aligned with Bill's approach. It's exactly the message that I want my sellers to hear. *The Digital Selling Handbook* is the most comprehensive manual that addresses the changes we've seen in customer buying patterns over recent years."

Chris Kelleher, Vice President, Americas Digital Sales
VMware

"Asynchronous selling is the future of this profession! Those who learn how to bring value and insight into the sales process before the customer even knows a problem exists will have the competitive advantage. Stinnett outlines the steps you need to take to win in the age of digital selling!"

Justin Geib, Vice President, US Sales
Dell Technologies

"Absolutely one of the best books I've read in a long time! This is not a typical sales training manual. The world of selling has completely changed in the last three to five years and this is your new guide to modern go-to-market strategy. I can't wait to put this in front of my sales and marketing teams as part of our required reading!"

Jeffrey Glahn, Senior Vice President, Head of Global Sales
TiVo Xperi

"With our customers now more geographically disparate, many people working from home, and travel budgets having been reduced, it seems everyone in business is simply more comfortable engaging virtually. Stinnett lays out the new paradigm for the activities and behaviors that will lead to success in our post-pandemic world. This book is a must read for my own sales organization and yours, too!"

Rachel Roberts, Vice President, Global Enterprise Sales
Cisco

"Digital transformation is radically changing industries, cultures, how we engage with customers, and how we live our lives. What remains is the need for authentic and meaningful connections centered on trust, credibility, and customer value. In *The Digital Selling Handbook*, Bill simplifies the complex and shares valuable insights and easy-to-use tools to help anyone in the relationship business elevate their personal brand and more effectively engage customers across all digital platforms. A must-read book for every sales, marketing, and business professional!"

Lynn Smullen, Senior VP, Global Strategic Clients Group
Oracle

"Even after experiencing the positive effects of his work with our teams over several years, I have to say, this is Stinnett's best contribution yet! Yesterday's approaches to sales communications are becoming increasingly ineffective. This book is a must for every B2B seller who wants to remain competitive and relevant."

Mike Ruhnke, Vice President, Enterprise Investment Accounts
Verizon Business

"This is not just an academic lecture; rather it's a complete 'how-to' guide to acquire more customers and close more deals in today's sales environment. It offers practical, real-world actions that anyone can take immediately. This book will be the perfect gift for my entire team!"

Mike Fouts, Vice President, Americas Partner Sales
Citrix

"Bill Stinnett nailed it! This book articulates the key tenets of success that I have relied on while leading high-performing sales teams on a regional, national, and global basis. Leveraging *The Digital Selling Handbook*, sales professionals will learn how to run their territory like a CEO and propel themselves to greater heights in the future. Well done!"

Jeffrey Harvey, SVP & Chief Revenue Officer, Industry Cloud
SAP

"A modern and fresh look at the art of selling and how digital enhances physical. Bill shows you how to lead the digital buying experience by providing knowledge and insights! This synopsis of selling in today's world was exactly what I was looking for."

Don Cooper, SVP, Partner Programs and Strategy
PTC

"In today's always-connected world, every salesperson needs to be a digital marketer. And learning how to leverage digital assets for sales is a must for every marketer. Stinnett lays out a plan for sales and marketing to be aligned and work better together to attract, convert, and close more business faster!"

Meenu Agarwal, Group SVP, Customer Experience and Success
Workday

"Bill Stinnett's work with our global sales teams has had a tremendous impact. But over the last several years we've seen tectonic changes in customer buying behavior. This new book comes at the perfect time! It provides a systematic and practical way to partner with clients the way they buy today. You'll want to take notes!"

Saso Kitanoski, President, Market Area Europe
Metso Outotec

"An excellent book written from the perspective of a highly experienced seller and sought-after sales trainer. Bill Stinnett lays out practical guidelines for selling in the digital world and explains how our sales motions have to evolve to succeed in this new era. Highly recommend!"

Charles Forsgard, Vice President, Global Sales
Honeywell Advanced Sensing Technologies

"Having worked with Bill Stinnett at four different companies since 2005, I can confidently say that *The Digital Selling Handbook* takes the best of the best of his concepts and tools and applies them to selling in our more virtual world. Don't go to market ill-equipped. Read this book!"

Marc Dyman, EVP, Kinetic Business and Wholesale
Windstream

"Today's best sales and marketing teams are empowering customers to make faster, more well-informed buying decisions using digital selling assets. *The Digital Selling Handbook* arrives at a perfect time to help you hone your current go-to-market strategy as you solidify trust and develop preference with your future customers."

Dino Perone, Group Vice President, Mid Market Sales
Spectrum Enterprise

"Digital selling is not just for inside sales anymore. Today, everybody is a digital seller . . . it's about building relationships and creating opportunities using digital channels. This book will cause a revelation for many sales and marketing teams and a revolution for many others."

Sid Kumar, Senior Vice President, Revenue Operations
HubSpot

"Bill Stinnett and his sales philosophy have been part of the way I lead sales teams since I read *Think Like Your Customer* in 2005. With *The Digital Selling Handbook*, Bill applies the idea of facilitating the customer's buying process to using digital selling assets to advance a deal toward closure even in between scheduled meetings with your customer. Brilliant!"

Peter Lindstrom, Director, Marking and Coding
Hitachi IESA

"Clear and concise wisdom and advice! Having seen Bill Stinnett in action, I understand why he's regarded as one of the best in the business helping both field sales and marketing teams make the transition from "old-school selling" to the more dynamic world of digital selling. Even seasoned and successful sales and marketing professionals will be challenged to take their game to the next level."

"A comprehensive educational tool for sales professionals and entrepreneurs alike! This book is a guide for enabling sales and customer support using digital mediums while applying Bill's *Think Like Your Customer* approach to the digital age!"

"*The Digital Selling Handbook* is an essential guide for every seller and marketer who wants to truly dominate in today's digital marketplace. The strategies Bill reveals about how to build e-relationships with buyers and move sales opportunities forward through every stage of the customer's buying process using digital assets is solid gold. An absolute must-read!"

"I've said it many times, Bill Stinnett is the best classroom sales trainer in the world! He's worked with our global sales teams on four continents! With this newest book, Bill shows every marketer and salesperson exactly what they need to know to thrive in the future of selling."

"It's been over a decade since I was introduced to Bill Stinnett and his philosophies of sales. His work with our team here in India and throughout the world has had a lasting impact. Now, I am thrilled to read *The Digital Selling Handbook*. This is essential for success in the digital age!"

"Spot on for today's selling environment! Bill Stinnett's new book is packed with extensive research, new ideas, and the latest digital selling strategies that build on his proven methodology, which I've been using with my sales teams since 2005. This is a critical resource for any salesperson whether just starting out or updating their existing approach."

Steve Miller, Director, Strategic Accounts
Videojet, a Danaher Company

"We started working with Bill Stinnett in 2009 with nine inside sales reps. We've now grown to over 400! With *The Digital Selling Handbook*, Bill gives you a full instruction how to build a selling machine for the digital world including the new norm of remote working from home, online chats, and video calls. A must read if you want to outplay your competitors and win more customers!"

Mikhail Penkovsky, VP, Inside Sales and Commercial Sales EMEA
Veeam

"Bill Stinnett's true gift is his ability to turn concepts into words that inspire readers to go out and take action. If you want to dominate in the marketplace of tomorrow, polish and perfect your digital selling skills. This book will give you the framework, then you'll have to put it into action. Step out. Be relevant. Be valuable. Be compelling. And leave your mark on the world!"

Jeff Bernier, Global Sales Director, New Emerging Technologies
Ansys

"This book is truly amazing and will change the sales journey by making salespeople more mindful of the experience they are giving their customers! It's super easy to read and apply. Bill's passion and enthusiasm for helping salespeople better serve their customers shines through in every word."

Kelli E Ballou-McMillan, Director, Global Channels
Five9

"A valuable handbook for sellers looking to spark meaningful conversations and allow customers to control the communication in our digital-first world. Follow Bill's approach to sales and marketing, and your business will stay ahead of the curve."

David Cancel, Executive Chairman
Drift

"Bill Stinnett is truly breaking new ground as *the* champion and thought leader on asynchronous selling. Our customers' buying journey is no longer a linear sequence of meetings with suppliers but a dynamic, self-directed exploration that happens largely without ever talking to anyone. Read this book and learn how to earn buyer preference and compress your sales cycle using digital selling assets and cutting-edge strategies."

Kevin McGrath, Vice President of Sales, Western Region
Sangoma

"A true business masterpiece! This is a modern treatise on how marketing and sales must work together in today's digital marketplace. Thought provoking and so well written, this book is a resource you'll want to come back to again and again."

Raquel Wiley, Vice President of Marketing
Netfortris

"Stinnett does a great job of addressing the challenges and the opportunities of the new world of digital selling. This book is a great "working guide" packed with practical suggestions to solutions that the readers can implement and use. I'll be buying copies for all my leaders!"

Rob Rosa, SVP, Global Service Sales & Customer Success
Extreme Networks

"Despite 30+ years of experience, I've quickly come to realize that digital selling is critical to everyone's success today, including mine! These principles and strategies are helping my team connect, engage, create trust, identify needs, position ourselves, and sell to customers using our smartphone and laptop in this new hybrid work model."

Mike Maiorana, Senior Vice President, Public Sector
Persado

"Bill Stinnett has been a go-to expert for our company since 2003. With *The Digital Selling Handbook*, he brings all of his tried-and-true concepts and applies them to the digital marketplace. At igus, our CEO says, "go digital or die." This book will show you exactly what to do to better align with how your customers seek out and research solutions today."

Joe Ciringione, VP of Sales, Energy Chain Systems
igus

"Quality face time with customers is getting harder to come by. They have grown accustomed to doing a lot of their discovery and online research on their own. Stinnett provides the guidance sellers need to engage with their clients earlier in the buying process, using both inbound and outbound methods, to attract and create more new sales opportunities."

Ray Himmel, Senior Vice President, Global Sales
VUV Analytics

"Stinnett is back with a profound new framework for empowering customers to work through their buying decisions almost entirely asynchronously. You'll learn how to become a trusted resource by providing digital content designed to shape the customer's thought process and help them *get ready to buy*. Great stuff!"

James Lattin, Professor of Marketing, Graduate School of Business
Stanford University

"Stinnett's deep understanding of customer psychology is indefectible. He beautifully articulates the way buyers research, find solutions to their problems, and make buying decisions in the digital world. Bill makes a very compelling case as to why we need to fully embrace modern communication tools, then provides a practical method to apply everything he teaches. I can't imagine a more useful book!"

Luc Wathieu, Professor of Marketing, McDonough School of Business
Georgetown University

"Long gone are the days when the majority of selling could be done face-to-face. Today's reality is that most of your selling needs to be done asynchronously. From the strategic creation of digital assets to the nurturing of e-relationships, to tactics for closing deals digitally, this book tells you everything you need to know for selling more effectively in the digital world. What a great follow-up to Stinnett's previous two bestsellers!"

Michel Tuan Pham, Professor of Business, Graduate School of Business
Columbia University

"An owner's manual for everyone that touches the revenue cycle, including Leadership, Infrastructure, Marketing, Support, Sales Enablement, Customer Service and Sales! My advice: read one chapter at a time, then act on what you've read!"

Anthony Parinello, *Wall Street Journal* Best-Selling Author
Creator of ***Selling to VITO, the Very Important Top Officer***

"As someone constantly preaching that sellers must be more proactive to create new opportunities, I absolutely love *The Digital Selling Handbook*. Bill does an amazing job blending the human side of selling into the deployment of the powerful digital tools available to modern sales pros. My favorite thing about this book is that it builds on the tried and true, proven fundamentals for developing new business instead of attempting to replace them!"

Mike Weinberg, Best-Selling Author
New Sales. Simplified. and ***Sales Management. Simplified.***

"Salespeople are often stereotyped as talkative. But selling and persuasion in the digital age is as much about writing as it is talking. In this book, Bill inspires us with this digital selling mindset and challenges us to learn to illuminate our thoughts and communicate with clients through digital channels."

Amri Tarsis, IoT Sales Director, Canada and Latin America
Cisco

"Talk about an idea whose time has come! *The Digital Selling Handbook* is exactly what the world of B2B sales and marketing needs to better align with how customers buy today. I've always believed sales is all about relationships. Today, we have to master how to build and grow those relationships digitally in between the more limited opportunities we have to meet with our customers in person."

Mark Smith, Regional Sales Manager, Healthcare Team
Oracle

"The rules of digital selling are rapidly evolving. *The Digital Selling Handbook* includes so much of what modern sellers need to know to earn a prospect's attention, their interest, and their business in today's crazy-busy, multi-screen, highly distracted world. I expect this book will be an often referenced and dog-eared guide for sellers going forward!"

Matt Heinz, President, **Heinz Marketing**
Host of **Sales Pipeline Radio**

"Digital communication with prospective clients is still highly underutilized in my opinion. This book gives an extremely comprehensive framework for those who are still trying to figure it out and those who want to sharpen the edges of their digital sword."

Dale Dupree, Founder and Chief Sales Officer
The Sales Rebellion

"This book had me at 'hello.' The fundamentals of working with people haven't and will not change; Sales is about helping people! But the rapidly evolving digital landscape has changed the game when it comes to where, when, and how buyers make purchasing decisions."

Amy Volas, Founder & CEO, **Avenue Talent Partners**
Co-Founder of **Thursday Night Sales**

"Bill Stinnett is an absolute genius when it comes to understanding and influencing how and why customers buy. In this complex digital marketplace, *The Digital Selling Handbook* is an essential guide for anyone involved in sales, marketing, and especially personal branding!"

Vanessa Carabelli, Co-founder of **Care-er Empowerment**
LinkedIn Top Voice, Latin America

THE
DIGITAL
SELLING
HANDBOOK

GROW YOUR SALES BY ENGAGING,

PROSPECTING, AND CONVERTING CUSTOMERS

THE WAY THEY BUY TODAY

BILL STINNETT

Mc Graw Hill

New York   Chicago   San Francisco   Athens   London   Madrid
Mexico City   Milan   New Delhi   Singapore   Sydney   Toronto

1 2 3 4 5 6 7 8 9   LCR   27 26 25 24 23 22

ISBN   978-1-264-27886-2
MHID   1-264-27886-1

e-ISBN   978-1-264-27887-9
e-MHID   1-264-27887-X

Library of Congress Cataloging-in-Publication Data

Names: Stinnett, Bill, author.
Title: The digital selling handbook : grow your sales by engaging, prospecting, and
    converting customers the way they buy today / Bill Stinnett.
Description: New York : McGraw Hill Education, [2022] | Includes bibliographical
    references and index.
Identifiers: LCCN 2022021502 (print) | LCCN 2022021503 (ebook) |
    ISBN 9781264278862 (hardback) | ISBN 9781264278879 (ebook)
Subjects: LCSH: Selling—Technological innovations. | Electronic commerce. |
    Internet marketing.
Classification: LCC HF5438.25 .S7469 2022 (print) | LCC HF5438.25 (ebook) |
    DDC 658.85—dc23/eng/20220504
LC record available at https://lccn.loc.gov/2022021502
LC ebook record available at https://lccn.loc.gov/2022021503

McGraw Hill books are available at special quantity discounts to use as premiums and sales promotions or for use in corporate training programs. To contact a representative, please visit the Contact Us pages at www.mhprofessional.com.

McGraw Hill is committed to making our products accessible to all learners. To learn more about the available support and accommodations we offer, please contact us at accessibility@mheducation.com. We also participate in the Access Text Network (www.accesstext.org), and ATN members may submit requests through ATN.

For Terri, Ashley, Ryan, Hannah, and David

Contents

Acknowledgments

What an honor it is to have the opportunity to thank so many people for the support and encouragement that ultimately led to starting and finishing this book. An undertaking like this couldn't possibly be completed alone.

First to my wife, Terri, and our four kids, Ashley, Ryan, Hannah, and David, as well as my father-in-law and mother-in-law, Jimmie and Karen. Thank you for keeping our world together as I took the time to immerse myself in this subject matter and learn enough about this topic to be able to create a work like this—not to mention spending so much time in the writing and editing process.

To the dedicated team at Sales Excellence: Where would I be without you? First a shout-out to Cortiney Bradley, my COO for the last seven years, whose fingerprints are found on pretty much every aspect of our business. Special thanks to both Dave Rohlf and Liz Shirey for their tireless efforts in making this content really sing. And to Kim Hannan and Franziska Moran for bringing these ideas to life online and putting up with one of the pickiest guys around.

I want to thank my dear friends and fellow Sales Excellence facilitators Cesar Dulong Neuman, Tony Bulleid, Chris Fergen, Timofei Rassokhin, and Michael Song. You've brought these ideas to so many people around the world in languages that I will never understand, let alone be able to speak. Thank you all for making Sales Excellence a special place to work.

I also owe a debt of gratitude to a great many special clients who have become much more than just customers but longtime friends. Some of these folks I've even had the honor of serving at multiple companies over the last 20 years. These include, but are by no means limited to, George Fischer, Mike Ruhnke, Jim Kilmer, Steve Springer, Andrea Connington,

Tiina Vuorenmaa, Saso Kitanoski, Marc Dyman, Padraig McDonnell, Scott Fulwider, Mike Harrington, Betsy Bear, Amri Tarsis, Michelle Accardi, Diego Santos Burgoa, Michelle Ruyle, Chris Whitaker, Michelle Hyde, Rick Abbate, Brad Barrett, Steve Miller, and Peter Lindstrom. A special thanks to Kuno van der Post for reaching out to literally ask me to write this book even before I knew I needed to.

I want to thank my editors at McGraw Hill, Donya Dickerson and Jonathan Sperling. Donya, you've been such a strong supporter and a friend since 2004. I dearly appreciate you! And Jonathan, you are truly one of the kindest and easiest to work with people I have ever known. Special thanks to Steve Straus for his outstanding work on the interior design.

Thank you to many great friends who have loved me and helped me in all areas of my life, including my longtime friend and confidant, Jeff Bernier; the best sales manager I ever worked for, Mark Smith; many of my brothers in Christ, Scott McKay, Alex Anderson, Franklin Crockett, Nathan Varn, and Phil Zaller; and my dear friend and spiritual mentor, Robby Spillman.

And last but not least, to YOU! The person who is reading these words right now. You are the reason I dedicated so much time, energy, and money in writing and promoting this work. You were my inspiration! Now it's up to you to take what you read here and put it to use. All my best to you and everyone you love!

Ellijay, Georgia
July 2022

Introduction

It's been almost 18 years since I had the privilege of publishing my first book, *Think Like Your Customer* (McGraw Hill 2005). It was truly the fulfillment of a lifelong dream! I didn't know it at the time, but that experience would change my life forever. That book was eventually translated into nine languages, and as I've traveled the world speaking and training for nearly two decades, I have been constantly amazed by how many people say they have benefited from reading it.

Two years later, I published *Selling Results!* (McGraw Hill 2007), which expanded on the first book and provided an extensive set of sales tools for applying many of those original ideas. It became the foundation of our *Sales Excellence® Core Methodology*, which has been adopted by organizations and individuals in over 40 countries. For an average kid from a tiny town in the mountains of Oregon, this whole journey has felt a bit surreal.

Of course, I always hoped all of this effort would produce some return-on-time-invested. But the personal satisfaction of seeing so many people apply these ideas to sell more, advance their careers, start businesses, and change their lives has been utterly overwhelming. I fully expected I would keep on publishing a new book every couple of years, but then something extraordinary happened: I got married!

I've often joked around by saying, "Number of books published before being married with kids = 2. Number of books published since being married with kids = 0." But I wouldn't change it for the world! I feel blessed beyond imagination to be married to my best friend, Terri. She is truly the love of my life! And we have the privilege of being parents to four wonderful kids. This time has been the most rewarding and satisfying period of my life. But now, after all these years, it's time to publish again. I'm like a rock band that finally got around to releasing their third album. Yay!

In this brief introduction, I want to answer four important questions that you might be asking:

1. Why do we need another book on sales?
2. Who is this book written for?
3. What is covered in this book?
4. What will this book do for me?

Let's take a look at these questions one at a time.

Why Do We Need Another Book on Sales?

Over the last 80 years or so, literally thousands of books have been written on sales and marketing. Why do we need another one? It's very simple: what the most effective salespeople and business owners are doing today to attract, prospect, convert, and close new sales opportunities has changed pretty substantially over the last few years. Oh, you can still use the same tactics you were using in 2019 to find and close some business today. You can even automate many of the sales motions you used to do by hand so you can dramatically scale the number of people you approach. But I'm just not comfortable with the only strategy for selling in today's market being simply "swing harder."

Seismic changes in the sociopolitical climate, the business landscape, as well as the rapid proliferation of communication technology have dramatically changed the way our customers explore solutions to their problems and work through a buying process. This means we really have no choice but to change the way we engage with them, or we will be summarily left in the dust.

Everything I write and create is based on personal, firsthand experience—learning and applying new ideas and new technologies on a daily and weekly basis. I am as involved in day-to-day selling as I was when I started my first direct sales job at age 22. I choose to be! How can I have any credibility helping other salespeople and business owners create and close new business in today's marketplace if I'm not doing it myself?

What I'm doing to forge new relationships and lead prospects through their discovery process today is dramatically different than what I was doing just a few years ago. I've read more, studied more, and experimented more in the last three years than I ever have in my life. In fact, I'd say about half of what's in this book I didn't even know 36 months ago. I'm going to share as much as I can of what I've learned about selling in today's digital-first world so you can benefit from it, too!

Who Is This Book Written For?

Before they publish anything, any good writer should think about exactly who their audience is going to be. They need to be able to answer this question: "Who's going to read this, and what will they be able to get out of it?" With that in mind, my target audience for this book is those people who fill a specific function with any or all of the following objectives:

- Influencing customer perception and persuading customers to draw new conclusions and literally think differently
- Communicating with customers—either verbally or in writing—via any given communication medium before, during, or after the sale
- Creating sales opportunities by helping customers conclude that they need help
- Demonstrating and presenting products and services as solutions to specific challenges that customers face
- Helping customers work their way through their own buying process from the earliest recognition of a need (or even before) all the way through closure and beyond
- Maintaining relationships with customers who bought—and even prospects who didn't—until the next opportunity to serve them comes along
- Leading or employing a team doing any of the above

With that in mind, the roles for which this book is perfectly suited include:

CEOs, presidents, CROs, and
VPs of sales

Marketing executives

Sales directors and managers

Account executives (AEs)

Sales development reps (SDRs)

Business development
reps (BDRs)

Account managers (AMs)

Channel sales managers

Customer success managers

Solutions architects and product
specialists

Pre-sales engineers and post-
sales consultants

Entrepreneurs and solopreneurs

Business owners and managers

Sole proprietors

Marketing professionals

Marketing consultants

Advertising agencies and
copywriters

Independent sales
representatives

Distributors, dealers, agents, and
resellers

Recruiters and staffing
professionals

Consultants and consulting
partners

I also hope to support—and even inspire—those in the role I like to call the "sales entrepreneur." These people usually come in one of two flavors. The first is made up of sales professionals working within a company who are willing to run their defined market or sales territory as if it were their own business. The term intrapreneur has become popular to describe a role where personal ownership of plans, strategies, and outcomes is encouraged.

I'll be talking much more about this throughout this book, but I believe that truly standing out in a world full of so much digital noise requires an individual to be willing to step up and build a personal brand as the go-to resource for their target customers. Sales professionals who approach their role like they're the CEO of their own company act and sound entirely differently than a typical "sales rep."

The second flavor of sales entrepreneur is the rapidly growing ranks of the independent sales contractor. In recent years, we have witnessed the phenomenon of record numbers of corporate professionals resigning their positions to start their own company. Just as many have started their own part-time business on top of working their day job.

Last year alone the number of new business applications filed in the United States was over 5.4 million, up over one million applicants from the previous year.[1] Futurists are now predicting that many more corporations will be moving toward a model where their sales teams will be composed primarily of self-employed subcontractors as opposed to direct (common law) employees.

We actually have two different but similar models for this already. One is the "manufacturers rep," which has been extremely popular for decades. This is especially common in industries like apparel, groceries, and hardware, where manufacturers engage a third-party representative to promote their products to regional distributors and local retailers, for example.

The other model, which is incredibly pervasive in the technology space, is one where solution providers offer their products and services through value-added resellers (VARs), dealers, agents, distributors, or the more generic term, *channel partners*. Some of the most successful technology companies in the world have built their business exclusively using the channel model, and Forrester Research recently released findings showing that a whopping 75 percent of all sales today flow through some form of distribution channel.[2]

The evolution toward what is being called the "gig economy," where individuals are contracted to perform specific tasks or complete defined projects, is becoming commonplace and will likely become more so within the arena of sales and marketing in the coming years. This model makes sense for self-employed sellers and marketers who want more control over where they work, when they work, work-life balance, etc. And it makes sense for many companies that want to reduce the risks and expense of hiring people directly as well as the liability and financial obligation of long-term employment. It's a win-win!

Whether you are a corporate employee, an entrepreneur selling solutions that your own company produces, or you are representing the goods and services of others, this book has been written with you in mind. I have endeavored to make this relevant to sales pros and business owners alike by combining my own background in corporate sales, my experience as a small business owner, and my knowledge from over 20 years working with a client base of companies ranging from one salesperson to thousands.

What Is Covered in This Book?

The scope of this work encompasses the best practices of selling digitally from the very earliest stages of a sales opportunity though closure and far beyond. It covers how we can use technology and digital assets to build and nurture what I like to call *e-relationships* with our past, present, and future clients.

I specifically chose not to go deep into an exposé of sales automation and enablement technologies for two major reasons. First of all, that's not my primary area of expertise. There are plenty of authors and experts who specialize in evaluating and recommending sales technology platforms. My work has always been more in the area of understanding how customers think and teaching sellers how to influence their customers' thinking and behavior throughout the overall buying process.

The second reason I won't spend a lot of time on the composition of your sales "tech stack," as it is frequently called, is that by the time this manuscript becomes available in bookstores or online, the technology and the players providing it will probably have changed substantially. The focus of this book is more on the substance of how you sell *using* technology, not the technology itself.

Here's just a tiny glimpse into what each chapter is about:

Chapter 1: *Selling the Way Customers Buy Today*

This first chapter is designed to lay the foundation of the topic of digital selling and why embracing it is so vitally urgent today. It also serves as a bit of an executive summary of the entire book. If you can only make time to carefully read the first chapter, you will walk away with a ton of new ideas that will cause you to reexamine how you sell in today's digital-first environment.

Chapter 2: *Engaging Customers Early in Their Digital Buying Process*

This covers how to connect and build relationships with prospective buyers long before a sales opportunity exists and, ideally, before they even know they need to consider buying something. We'd ultimately like to be the company that is helping individuals and organizations conclude that they need our help in the first place and in so doing become the benchmark to which all other would-be providers are compared.

Chapter 3: *Mastering Digital Selling and Content Development*

The third chapter is about writing and creating sales content. If you are familiar with the term *content marketing*, you know the power of engaging prospective buyers by educating and informing them as opposed to just advertising to them. Selling with content is a way to help customers reach specific conclusions that are part of their overall buying and decision-making processes. We use content to do the same selling we would do if we were meeting with them in person. I assure you, this approach is a total game changer!

Chapter 4: *Designing Your Digital Selling Engine*

Here's where we dig into the various platforms and tools you can employ as part of your overall digital selling strategy. We'll look at the various kinds of technologies you can use to attract, connect with, converse with, and communicate digitally with customers, including several of the most popular platforms available at the time of this writing.

Chapter 5: *Building e-Relationships Throughout the Digital Buying Journey*

This chapter contains as many strategies, tactics, tips, and techniques as I could pack into it. We'll talk about how to lead prospective clients from being a total stranger, to a social connection, to having a live conversation. Then we'll talk about how to convert them to happy repeat customers and even market ambassadors helping you get the word out to other people who can potentially use your help.

Chapter 6: *Creating a Magnetic Personal Brand*

This is my favorite chapter! In today's digital marketplace, it's not easy to stand out among so many other voices vying for your customer's attention. The key is to differentiate yourself by letting your customers get to know who you are as you earn trust, credibility, and preference for doing business with you. If you start to lose momentum as you read, make sure you get to Chapter 6 before you run out of gas. You don't want to miss it!

Chapter 7: *Sales Prospecting in a Digital World*

For those who are responsible for outbound prospecting, I have laced every chapter of this book with highly actionable ideas and advice for you. But Chapter 7 is where we go deep into the strategy of targeted prospecting with ideas about how to approach senior executives and how to create a 30-day prospecting plan. There's even a section on the psychology of overcoming what's keeping you from doing the prospecting you already know you need to be doing.

Chapter 8: *Managing and Closing Deals Digitally*

Digital selling is often thought of as technology-powered prospecting and using social media for lead generation. In this final chapter, we will explore how to use digital assets and the latest communication platforms to move opportunities forward through all stages of the customer's buying process, even when you don't have the opportunity to talk to all of the key stakeholders in person, on video, or via telephone.

What Will This Book Do for Me?

The purpose of this book is to intentionally change the way you think about the profession of selling and how you communicate with your prospective clients in today's digital world. We're going to explore a variety of ways to leverage digital communication channels throughout the entire marketing and sales process. You'll learn how to:

- Find and create more new sales opportunities using the latest in digital selling technologies.

- Influence perception about the value you can deliver for prospective buyers in your market to generate demand for what you offer.

- Build relationships and rapport with prospective clients even before they know they need anything.

- Align and position your products and services in the mind of your customers as the ideal solution to help them achieve the goals they already want to achieve.

- Write better emails, social posts, articles, and other digital assets that can be used to attract prospective clients and the substance of your prospecting outreach.

- Leverage the latest in social and other digital technologies using a variety of media to reach and develop connections with an unlimited number of potential customers.

- Foster relationships with prospective buyers who are ready to buy today as well as earn trust with those who may be prospects in the future.

- Establish yourself as a resource for information and answers that draws prospective clients to you when they need your knowledge and expertise.

- Put together a strategy for reaching out to targeted prospective clients that is designed to help you stand out from the crowd and get you noticed.

- Improve your average win rate and close more of the sales opportunities that you choose to invest your time in.

* * *

Before we step into the first chapter, I want to congratulate you for taking this initiative. At a time when some companies are cutting back on investing in career development for their sales teams, I applaud you for making the time to invest in yourself! If you are a business owner, you already know that you have to make yourself better if you want to achieve better results. And if you are leading an organization, this is an opportunity to capture a vision of what's possible for your team at the next level.

What's in this book represents a departure from many of the tired, outmoded sales and marketing practices of yesteryear. I'm on a mission to eradicate *bad selling* that is simply being automated and executed "at scale." You are about to be challenged to completely rethink how you *sell* using digital media for communicating with your customers.

Let's go!

THE
DIGITAL
SELLING
HANDBOOK

CHAPTER 1

Selling the Way Customers Buy Today

As a guy who's been around sales and entrepreneurship for a while, I can confidently say that the foundational truths of selling have never changed and they never will. At its root, business involves a buyer who needs or wants something and is willing to trade either money or something else of value to a seller who can provide it. Marketing and sales are simply what the selling party does to try to find or attract a prospective buyer and then facilitate the transaction.

This simple definition applies far beyond what most would consider traditional sales and marketing. It describes just about anyone who promotes, endorses, or recommends anything to anybody. In today's world, the vast majority of that promoting, recommending, and selling happens digitally.

Whether you are a sales or marketing professional in a large corporation, an entrepreneur running your own company, or even a volunteer seeking support and donations for a nonprofit organization, you're selling, whether you charge money or not! Selling and persuasion are natural and vital components of how we function as a society. As Thomas Watson, longtime CEO and chairman of IBM, put it, "Nothing happens until somebody sells something."

Throughout this book I'll use terms like *seller* and *buyer, salesperson* and *customer,* or *supplier* and *channel partner,* but what I'll be describing is the relationship between any two people or entities on either end of an exchange. One of them promotes and delivers a product or service. The other consumes or resells that product or service, which could actually be a subscription, a membership, or just the adoption of some idea or opinion.

Unfortunately, a myriad of research studies—as well as the personal experiences of anybody selling pretty much anything in the modern world—reveal that today's would-be customers are becoming increasingly sales averse. That's entirely understandable! Every one of us is being sold to all day long every day on billboards, TV, radio, podcasts, Facebook, YouTube, and even at every gas pump! If you stand still for even a few seconds, somebody will try to pitch you on something.

As selling and promotion have become more automated and mechanical, prospective buyers have become more closed and guarded. People are mastering the art of avoiding advertisements, screening phone calls, and ignoring unsolicited correspondence. They are more and more resistant to engaging in a live sales conversation that they themselves did not initiate. That means those of us who make a living promoting a product, a service, a skill, or an idea will have to adapt to survive.

The Way Customers Buy Today

In years past, salespeople had far more latitude and opportunity to connect and meet with their customers face-to-face. Meetings at the client's office, trade shows, industry events, meeting up for coffee, business lunches, networking groups, tickets to sporting events: for decades these were the norm. More recently, salespeople have seen a sharp decline in the number of opportunities to spend quality time with prospective clients for a variety of reasons.

Over the last decade or more, many companies have begun adopting policies that don't allow their employees to accept free meals, trips, or entertainment of any kind to avoid any appearance of impropriety. Over the past few years community health guidelines put severe restrictions in place that left the majority of people in many industries working from home. As a result, the business world had no choice but to adopt a variety of virtual communication tools and collaboration platforms. This obviously produced a massive shift in the way businesspeople interact with each other and with their customers.

One could argue those restrictions simply accelerated the natural adoption of live-video and other virtual collaboration tools that businesses would have eventually embraced anyway. But the long-term effects of that experience have left a huge percentage of people far less willing to meet with a salesperson face-to-face and, interestingly enough, even less likely to have a conversation via live-video or telephone. That is unless they have already determined that they might need some help that the salesperson's company can provide.

The majority of today's buyers show a strong preference for digital inter-actions, whether to avoid health risks, reduce the use of fossil fuels, save time, or simply to not have to change out of their pajamas. With less and less opportunity for personal interactions, we have to reimagine how we get to know our customers and how we enable our customers to get to know *us*.

According to the latest research from Gartner, only 17 percent of the time a B2B buyer invests in a buying process is spent engaging with poten-tial suppliers.[1] Another 27 percent of their time consists of doing online research, 22 percent meeting with their internal buying group, and 18 per-cent doing independent research offline. The balance includes other tasks like obtaining approvals and purchasing. This is illustrated in the graph in Figure 1.1.

Figure 1.1   Distribution of Buying Groups' Time by Key Buying Activities[2]

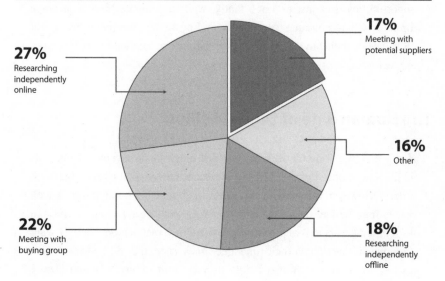

17%
Meeting with
potential suppliers

27%
Researching
independently
online

16%
Other

22%
Meeting with
buying group

18%
Researching
independently
offline

Now, if that buying group happens to be talking with and vetting three different would-be suppliers, that means each vendor could get as little as 5 or 6 percent of the customer's time and attention. The overwhelming majority of the time our customers invest in their buying process is not spent talking to us. Rather, it involves collecting, analyzing, and discussing information and ideas from who knows what sources while we're not even around.

This means . . .

If we're not willing to leverage digital media to continue selling in between the few meetings we *are* able to get with our customers, we lose the ability to influence perception and help them draw favorable conclusions during 94 percent of their buying process.

If that doesn't get your attention, I'm not sure what will! This kind of modern-day reality makes the topic of digital selling worth taking seriously, wouldn't you say?

This book will be an exploration of how to use a variety of digital communication platforms to attract prospective clients and create new sales opportunities. But just as importantly, we'll investigate how to leverage digital assets to continue to influence and persuade customers throughout all stages of their buying process, whether we are granted the opportunity to meet with them or not.

The Human Side of Digital Selling

Here's an interesting bit of irony: the vast majority of buyers—as many as 92 percent in one study—express a preference for virtual interactions with sellers.[3] However, the same buyers report an interest in doing business with real human beings they can relate to. Your prospective clients need and want real answers to real problems provided by a real person, but they want it on their terms and on their timetable. In essence, they'd like to feel what it's like to be your customer before they commit to anything and ideally without even talking to you.

Now more than ever, people are attracted to individuals and brands that share their values. Modern buyers crave authentic human interactions with sellers who are genuine. They are inundated with communication and advertising impressions but at the same time starved for actual care and attention.

**It seems the more virtual our world becomes,
the more we appreciate what's "real."**

What makes sellers attractive is their willingness to provide knowledge and information that helps would-be customers make decisions and draw conclusions on their own. Buyers seem to look at every potential supplier and ask more than just, "Can you sell me _____ (fill in the blank)?" They want to know, "How can you actually help me decide what I need to buy?" and "What else can you provide beyond just the commercial transaction that will help me?" It seems guidance and advice have become just as powerful differentiators as features and pricing.

All the anecdotal and empirical evidence shows that . . .

**Serving is the new selling! Today's buyers are
looking for more than just a source to buy from.
They want a resource to learn from!**

From my seat as a sales and marketing consultant and trainer to some of the world's most well-known organizations, the biggest mistake I see companies make is throwing their resources behind digital marketing and social channels to deliver the same old, worn-out, seller-centric "message" that their customers have been numb to for years.

Here's an idea worth remembering. . .

**Your customers have not only changed *where*
they buy; they have changed *how* they buy. Don't
approach today's communication channels with
yesterday's sales and marketing strategy.**

If effective marketing today was simply a matter of switching advertising channels, from print ads in magazines to LinkedIn ads, for example, that would be easy. If outside salespeople could suddenly fill their pipelines to overflowing just by embedding a short video into their emails or maybe sending a video via direct message through LinkedIn, there would be no need for a lot of what's in this book.

Granted, changing the medium or delivery mechanism of your outreach can measurably improve results. We'll be talking extensively about that as we go. But I honestly believe . . .

The big opportunity today lies in radically changing what is written or said *within* your sales and marketing message, *not* just how you deliver it.

The substance of what you communicate digitally has the power to influence and persuade. It can also give your prospects a glimpse of who you are as a person when it's designed to do so. A big part of digital selling is empowering your customers to learn about you and how you can help them even before you have any personal interaction with them. We'll talk much more about this in the coming chapters.

Eight Truths About Digital Selling

As I see it, there are at least eight truths that help distinguish digital selling from whatever we want to call the kind of selling we did before everything went digital. Let's briefly talk about each one of these truths to further define what digital selling is and what we need to do to embrace it.

1. Digital Selling Is for Anybody Who Is Promoting Anything

Admittedly, not *all* marketing and promotion today is digital. Traditional media are still alive and well in many industries. They would be defined as channels that existed before the rise of the internet, which includes newspapers, magazines, billboards, radio, broadcast TV, and direct mail. But nearly every business in the modern world, with the exception of something like a roadside stand, is using one or more forms of digital media to attract or transact with their customers. This includes everything you see online: websites, search engines, digital advertising, social media, video streaming services, online discussion forums, and even Google Maps displaying a business profile.

Digital buying goes far beyond just ordering books, or shoes, or groceries. The latest studies show that as much as 98 percent of all enterprise purchases—even capital expenditures and long-term contracts—start with online research, even if the transaction itself happens offline.[4] Our customers aren't just using the internet for their up front research. The Gartner Future of Sales 2025 report predicts that by 2025, 80 percent of sales interactions between buyers and sellers even in the business-to-business space will occur through digital channels.[5]

Here's another startling reality: The average person spends nearly six hours a day on their smartphone.[6] That's over 90 full days of the year! If you factor in an average of eight hours of sleep per night, we are spending over 37 percent of our waking moments—or every hour we're awake from January 1 through May 15—on our phone. Heaven help us!

In light of the way we live today, I think we can easily conclude . . .

**If your prospective customers can't find you
or get to know more about you from their
smartphone, you basically don't exist.**

Whether you are selling enterprise IT solutions in a corporate environment, running your own advertising agency, thinking about planting a church, or offering guitar lessons as a side hustle, digital selling is not merely an option. It's the way business and promotion is done today.

2. Digital Selling Exists to Facilitate Digital Buying

Because of the way modern customers buy, the art of selling has been forced to evolve. By and large, today's consumers prefer to operate in *stealth mode* whenever they seek out a solution to a problem or challenge. They explore options and potential suppliers and digitally "stalk" companies and individuals as part of their due diligence. And they do it all without talking to anyone. They are educating themselves and drawing conclusions based on what they can find online. Let's explore this a bit.

If your customers are resistant to scheduling an introductory telephone call; if they prefer to keep themselves current on new technologies and services through industry-specific podcasts, Facebook groups, and TED talks; and if they'd rather watch a YouTube video on a specific topic than speak with a salesperson, here's my question: Who's making those videos? Who's writing those posts? Who's actively engaging with your potential market on social media and providing educational and perception-forming video content and articles? Is it you? Or your competitors?

Think about it like this: If other companies in your industry are helping shift market perception by investing time and energy to meet prospective customers where they are (on their smartphones), who are those customers going to call when they are ready to talk? With whom will they be willing to book a 15-minute introductory telephone call?

It only makes sense that whoever is helping your prospective customers understand how they can improve their business and their lives by adopting the very products and services *you* sell is the one who earns the credibility and the trust needed to get to the live conversation stage when the time comes.

I think it's crucial to remember that . . .

> **In today's world, we have to leverage technology to
> empower prospective clients to make digital buying
> decisions on their choice of media 24/7/365.**

We're not just talking about one-to-one correspondence via email, text, or instant messaging. The kinds of digital conversations I'm referring to include the variety of one-to-many or many-to-many discussions that are happening in the modern digital marketplace. We have to learn how to make an active contribution to the conversations our customers are having with their peers and other influencers online.

We need to make it possible for an unlimited number of buyers located anywhere in the world to be able to discover us, because . . .

One of the key objectives of digital selling is to develop e-relationships with prospective customers as we empower them to come to know, like, and trust us before they ever have a chance to meet us.

This is the heart of building your business and expanding your influence in today's world. We'll be exploring exactly how to do this as we go!

3. Digital Selling Often Combines Inbound and Outbound Strategies

Not all that long ago we used the term *marketing* to describe the combination of efforts used to educate the marketplace, build brand awareness, attract prospective clients, and generate leads that were then handed off to a salesperson to follow up. *Prospecting* was what we called a salesperson reaching out directly to a client to try to start a conversation. Somewhere along the way the business world adopted two new terms: *inbound* to describe a lot of those traditional marketing functions designed to help prospective buyers find us, and *outbound* to describe what a salesperson does to find prospective buyers and connect with them.

Depending on whether you are a solopreneur, a business owner, or a sales pro working for a large company, you may have a team of other people working with you to execute your broader sales and marketing strategy. Consequently, your role and responsibilities for overall lead and demand generation will vary. But please take a moment to read this list of the channels most often employed for both inbound and outbound. As you read, think about how you and your company are currently using each of these:

Inbound

- Website SEO (search engine optimization)
- Paid search advertising and retargeting ads
- Organic social media posts and engagement
- Paid social media advertising

- Blogs, articles, books, and e-books
- Podcasts, webinars, and live-video broadcasts
- Online text-based, live-audio, and live-video discussion forums
- Every form of traditional nondigital advertising mentioned earlier

Outbound

- Direct postal or express mail
- Telephone calls and voicemail
- Manual and automated email
- Direct messaging via social platforms
- Text (smartphone) messaging
- Networking and industry events (live or online)
- Dropping by in person

If, by chance, you yawned as you read these lists, thinking, "I've seen this all before," I pose to you the following questions:

1. Which of these forms of media are you currently ignoring?
2. How many can you afford to continue to neglect?
3. Which of these is your competitor currently leveraging to attract, connect with, and make sales to your prospects without you even knowing about it?
4. Which one or more of these channels deserves some of your attention right now?

I seldom recommend that any company try to master all of these, certainly not all at once. But one of the secrets of digital selling, which should *not* be a secret, is that for every additional medium or communication channel you add, either inbound or outbound, the likelihood of recognition and connection increases substantially.

When someone sees your email related to solving the same business problem they saw you or your company talking about in a YouTube pre-roll ad the day before, that drives an entirely different level of recognition and attention than an email sequence or video advertisement alone. The key is to pick one or two of these media that you are currently underutilizing, add it to your repertoire, and decide to "own it" over the next 6 to 12 months. Then, add another one or two when it makes sense as you expand your reach.

I'm often asked, "Which medium is best?" My answer is, "Any and all you *believe* will work and that prove they can produce results." Now it's true that you may not know which ones to have faith in or which will work in your market until you invest some time and energy to test them.

But please consider this . . .

> **If you restrict your digital selling efforts to a single medium of communication—regardless of which it is—you could be missing 90 percent of your potential to connect with prospective buyers.**

Strategic experimentation and testing are vital. Mix it up and constantly test and tweak your approach. If you are using the exact same business development methods you were using two years ago, you're probably stuck in a comfort zone and are unwittingly stunting your potential growth.

For many companies that can attract, transact, and deliver entirely digitally with little to no human contact, an inbound-only strategy can be extremely successful and cost-effective. Good examples would include traditional and online retailers, inexpensive SaaS (software as a service) providers, online education, and other self-service offerings. However, if at some point the buyer has to get on the phone, videoconference, or meet face-to-face to complete a transaction or take delivery of your product or service, you can combine inbound attraction with outbound prospecting strategies for the ultimate one-two punch.

You might see the occasional headline proclaiming, "Outbound Prospecting Is Dead." Nonsense! Statements like that usually come from companies selling inbound lead-generation platforms, digital marketing services, or a course on social media advertising. But it is true that outbound efforts that are not supported by a strong inbound strategy are producing fewer and fewer results every year.

We'll talk much more about both inbound and outbound initiatives in later chapters, and we'll explore which ones might be best for you. I'll take the opportunity here to simply say that the majority of B2B settings, as well as most medium-to-big-ticket B2C sales environments, call for a creative combination of the two.

4. Digital Selling Is Predominantly Asynchronous

If you look again at the list of inbound and outbound media mentioned previously, you'll notice that on the inbound side only live-audio and live-video discussion forums represent real-time communication with a prospective buyer. Even on the outbound side, only telephone calls, networking events, and "dropping by" provide the chance to actually talk with prospective clients live. These kinds of opportunities for real-time customer engagement are frequently referred to as *synchronous selling*, where the buyer and the seller are interacting with each other simultaneously.

Every other medium or channel listed represents what we will call *asynchronous selling*. This includes all the situations where we would write or record something that our customer would read, watch, or listen to some number of minutes, days, or even years later.

It's important to acknowledge . . .

The majority of digital selling is done asynchronously!
Whether we like it or not, this is the future of
selling because it's the future of buying.

Actually, it's not only the future; it's the present!

Honestly, I'd rather just call people on the phone or drive over and meet with them, wouldn't you? I really miss those good old days! I even recently heard one well-known sales guru on a podcast saying, "I'm just a synchronous guy. That's who I am. I sell by talking to people!" Well, I suppose that's fine for anyone who's willing to render themselves irrelevant for the majority of buyers in today's market, who are going to find answers to their questions and make buying choices without talking to anyone.

Let's be absolutely clear: synchronous, real-time selling is definitely superior! When it comes to influencing perception and persuasion, nothing beats an in-person meeting. Live video is second best, followed by a telephone call. There are even certain steps in a complex sales cycle where I believe a synchronous conversation is flat-out required. We'll get into the details of that in Chapter 8.

What we have to decide is whether we're going to empower our prospective customers with the insight and information they need to draw smart conclusions asynchronously or watch them make buying decisions based on whatever else they can find on the internet.

Especially in the early stages of their exploration process, today's buyers strongly favor a more self-directed, asynchronous approach to buying for several reasons:

1. **They truly don't have time.** Many buyers are slammed wall-to-wall on video calls all day long. They're not inclined to schedule yet another meeting when they think they can just as easily gain some insight and answers to their questions with a simple Google or YouTube search or an inquiry post to their peers in a LinkedIn group.

2. **They want to maintain control.** Anybody who's not ready to buy right now—and even many who are—want to keep a certain distance from a salesperson so they can disengage anytime they choose without the embarrassment or the social pressure of canceling or telling someone no.

3. **They demand convenience.** Customers today get some of their best online "exploring" done late at night after everyone else in the house is asleep, while sitting in their car in a fast-food pickup line, or during a particularly uninteresting but required internal videoconference. They want to be able to access information whenever and wherever they choose.

There is little room in today's marketplace for sellers who insist on a telephone call or videoconference as the *only* way to start a sales conversation or advance a buying process. Your customers have too many other choices of people to work with and sources of information who *are* willing to engage digitally.

Please circle this, underline it, and put a star next to it ...

> **If the *only* objective of our asynchronous sales efforts is to try to book a synchronous conversation, we are totally missing the true potential of digital selling.**

Only a small fraction of the prospective customers in any market are ready or willing to get on the phone with you right now. It's what you say and ask in those early-stage asynchronous digital communications that leads people to the place where they are willing to get on the phone or videoconference with you when the time comes. If your digital selling is effective enough, you'll help your customer move one or more steps in your direction. Ideally, they will soon be calling *you* to request the appointment to speak on videoconference!

We're going to delve deep into this as we move forward, but I just can't resist making one of the most important points of this entire book right now ...

> **The true art of digital selling is proactively influencing perception and helping customers draw favorable conclusions about us before and after any real-time conversations!**

In the coming chapters, we'll be exploring how to help customers recognize their need for what we offer, communicate a value promise, and help them conclude that we are the best choice for them to explore moving forward with. And we'll learn how to do all of that without ever talking to our prospective client, if we have to.

This is usually the point where some sales and marketing leaders who are stuck in the past tell me, "That's not possible!" Sadly, they'll soon be watching their competitors—who are willing to embrace and apply what's in this book—do all of these things and much more entirely digitally.

5. Digital Selling Is More Than Just "Social Selling"

Earlier, we talked about the average person spending more than six hours a day on their smartphone. What's really mind-blowing is nearly two-and-a-half hours of that is spent on social media, and approximately half of that time (one out of every five minutes an average person spends on a smartphone) is on Facebook.[7] Of course, millions of people never use Facebook, and millions of others probably never shut it off, so averages can be deceiving. But there's no denying this: if you want to get in front of a lot of people these days, social media is a great place to do it.

A commitment to a strong social media strategy is one of the best ways to produce a consistent flow of new connections with prospective clients, but it's certainly not the only way. A daily or weekly show on a YouTube channel that is subsequently released as a podcast is another spectacular mechanism for building a loyal following today. There are a variety of other approaches we'll get to later.

Despite the amount of time people spend on platforms like Facebook or LinkedIn, 68 percent of online buying experiences that result in a purchase begin on a search engine.[8] The difference is "buyer intent." People go to a search engine to do research, get answers to their questions, or find something that they need. If they already know they need to buy something, a search engine is the quickest way to find someone who can provide it. People who are "buying now" use search!

People don't log on to Facebook to buy things or be subjected to marketing. They go there to wish their friends a happy birthday and see the latest pictures of their neighbor's baby. But a platform like Facebook is the perfect place to deliver a carefully crafted bit of insight or knowledge about what matters most to your target customers when they least expect it.

People don't go to LinkedIn to be sold to, either. They go there to find a job, network with like-minded people, and most importantly, to find prospects to whom they can sell *their own* products or services. A large percentage of the people who initiate connections or accept your requests to connect on LinkedIn are actually prospecting *you*! But if your approach is right, LinkedIn is still one of the best places to build e-relationships and create a social following of people who share an interest in the kinds of business outcomes you can deliver.

Like any good social-selling method, this book will cover building a red-hot social profile that is designed to convert visitors into followers, initiate sales conversations, and drive a steady stream of traffic to your door. But while most other programs focus primarily on making social connections and driving conversations, this is only the first layer of our overall process. We're going several layers deeper than that.

We're going to study the psychology of what drives people to take action and buy in the first place as well as what causes customers to choose one supplier over another. Then we're going to look at how to build that into your overall social strategy and the stories that you tell through your profile, your posts, your comments, your direct messages, and every other facet of your overall digital selling strategy.

Those of you who sell in a more complex environment—where there is still a lot of selling to be done *after* you receive an inquiry—will learn how to leverage a variety of digital assets to convert more of those leads into viable sales opportunities. Then you'll learn how to direct and manage those opportunities using additional creative digital assets throughout the sales process to close more business and maximize your revenue results.

6. Digital Selling Is Not Just Online Advertising

Some might think that digital selling is just a different name for banner ads, search engine advertising, YouTube pre-roll videos, and sponsored social posts, but it actually encompasses far more than just online advertising. Digital selling and persuasion also involves defining the *intent* of any organic or paid placement. The idea is not to just get your logo in front of more eyeballs but to literally change the beliefs and perceptions of the people who read, listen to, or watch what you publish.

Webster's dictionary offers us this definition of *advertising*: "the action of calling something to the attention of the public especially by paid announcements."[9] Most would agree the vast majority of advertising is just that: "calling attention." But drawing attention to our brand or our product is one thing. Helping a prospective client conclude that we could help them solve a business problem they have—or maybe even helping them realize they have a problem they didn't *know* they had—is quite another.

In the next chapter, we'll be talking about the difference between advertising and insight. Most advertising tends to focus on letting people know we are here if they need us. Insight, when properly delivered, is more about helping people draw the conclusion that they might have a need for us in the first place and helping them determine that we are the organization best suited to fill that need.

I want to save the real meat of this topic for the next chapter, but the point I'll make here is . . .

Digital selling is much more than just building awareness; it's about literally changing what your readers or viewers believe about you and, more importantly, what they believe about themselves.

To do this, we have to focus less on ourselves and start to focus on what our customers would get out of a relationship with our company. We have to sell by telling stories about how our prospective customers can derive measurable value by partnering with us. A powerful brand is one that tells a story in which the prospective customer is the protagonist! In our story, the customer becomes the hero who, with our help, overcomes all the obstacles and gets the desired outcome or result they already want.

How much of what's on your website, in your LinkedIn posts, or in your outbound emails is about you as opposed to the person you hope will read them? When you look at your own advertising, is it mostly about what you do? Or is it about what *your customer* can do with your help? The shift from "advertising" to digital persuasion through sharing insight and storytelling represents a huge departure from the majority of what we see and hear around us every day.

7. Digital Selling Is Done Primarily in Writing, Audio, or Video

As mentioned earlier, the majority of the time people spend during their exploration and buying process these days is asynchronous. They tend to do things like read websites, watch videos, and listen to podcasts at odd times between the other events in their day (or night). It's not that they may never meet with you or speak with you live by phone. It's that they may not be willing to talk live until they have read your LinkedIn profile, skimmed through a white paper your company published, or watched a short introductory video you sent them first. They might need a little more information before they decide if it's worth their time to talk to you!

An enormous percentage of digital selling is done using the written word, infographics, audio, and video. That means a lot of the "selling" we do in the future will be less about talking to people and more about engaging in what I like to call *e-conversations* across the internet. Much of the time, we'll be engaging people we don't yet know in one-to-many e-conversations via blogs, social media posts, automated email, podcasts, etc. I believe the aptitude to sell verbally will always be in demand and is still one of the most valuable skill sets in the world. But getting a scheduled appointment so you *can* sell verbally often requires great writing skills.

For decades, I professed that the most coveted competency a salesperson or marketer could ever develop—the one that could catapult their career to the next level more than any other—was public speaking. I still believe that facing and overcoming the fear of speaking in front of a group can do wonders for a person's confidence and self-esteem. Over the years I have seen people's lives and careers transformed after they complete our executive presentation skills workshops. But the most indispensable skill for selling in *today's* marketplace is not talking. It's the ability to influence, persuade, and sell via the written word.

Anyone who intends to stay relevant over the next five to ten years—or maybe even the next two—should commit to learning more about the art and science of *copywriting.* I'll admit, just a few years ago I didn't even know exactly what that term meant. Writing "sales copy" is basically using words to create digital assets, such as:

1. Social media profiles and posts

2. Subject lines and the body text of emails

3. Scripts or talking points for telephone calls or voicemails

4. Scripts or talking points for prospecting or educational videos

5. Websites, landing pages, or any other mechanism to convert visitors into leads or customers

6. A wide variety of sales assets we can use to do the selling for us when the customer isn't willing or able to talk to us in real time

The value of writing compelling copy cannot be overstated, because . . .

Effective writing is quickly becoming the difference between those who have the "gift of gab"—but very few appointments to use it—versus those who are able to seize the attention of today's busy customers *in writing* before they quickly swipe, delete, or click away.

Historically, the practice of copywriting has been reserved for advertisers and other professional writers. But today, every salesperson, marketeer, or small business owner desperately needs a variety of digital selling assets like those just listed. If you can hire someone else to write them for you, that's great. But you'll also need the ability to craft compelling emails, texts, and direct messages on the fly. If you want to begin to foster closer relationships with your readers, you'll also need to capture your own voice, expertise, and personality and weave that into what you write. Of course, you can get someone to help you if it makes sense. Every marketing department needs to be actively engaged in helping create digital selling assets that salespeople can quickly and easily leverage. But I also encourage every professional seller to learn to create these kinds of digital assets themselves!

I believe this so strongly that I've even created an online course called *Copywriting for Sales Professionals* to help those who want to improve the effectiveness of their sales writing. If that topic sounds interesting, you can download a free tip sheet on writing more compelling sales copy, which is based on major themes of that course, at: www.salesexcellence .com/handbook.

8. Digital Selling Is Not Just a Job for the Marketing Department

Some who read this will think, "Well, Bill, if our marketing department had a better SEO strategy, a stronger LinkedIn presence, or a more customer-outcome-focused email campaign, it would be a lot easier for our salespeople to book meetings." No doubt! I'm sure you're absolutely right! I've yet to see a marketing organization that couldn't—or didn't want to— do a better job of attracting clients than they are doing today.

But here's the thing . . .

> **Very few salespeople will ever have the luxury of a marketing team that supplies all the qualified leads they will ever need. You'll probably have to create at least some of your opportunities yourself!**

Of course, you can outsource the telemarketing function. You can build a team of sales development representatives (SDRs) or create an inside sales department to do a lot of the day-to-day outreach to prospects. But some aspects of prospecting, business development, networking, and referrals will *always* be the responsibility of the salesperson who "owns" the territory or the entrepreneur running the small business. Whether we like it or not—or think we have time for it or not—digital selling is not just a job for the marketing department.

Part of what is required to stand out in the marketplace can only be done by those who have the business acumen and the sales experience to open doors to hard-to-reach executives. That's good news! That means you and I will never become obsolete. I personally believe that today's sales professionals and business owners need to be as much demand generators as closers. This is especially true if you want to leverage social media or other platforms to build a magnetic personal brand that enables your best prospects to find you, which we'll be talking about in Chapter 6.

* * *

As we step forward, I want to point out that the contents of this book are not organized by platform or medium. You won't see a chapter dedicated to using video for business development or a separate chapter on how to use LinkedIn. Both of those are simply tools we can employ in a wide variety of ways to accomplish any given objective. The use of social media, YouTube, email, text messaging, and others will be referenced in nearly every chapter as it relates to the subject matter at hand.

This book is outlined around the major competency areas of digital selling. Each chapter builds on the last, but it's organized as a *handbook* so you can use it as a reference guide for any of these topics as you see fit. So go ahead, thumb through it if you want. Read some of the bolded callouts that are designed to highlight many of the most important takeaways as they draw you into the material wherever you happen to turn.

I absolutely believe you would benefit most by reading every chapter sequentially. But the book is in your hands now, so you can decide! Feel free to read page-by-page or jump around as you see fit. No matter how you choose to consume it, I hope you will devour what's here and start putting it to use immediately. I'm confident you won't be disappointed.

Putting These Ideas into Practice

Here are several actionable steps you can take to start to put some of these ideas to use right now:

1. *Assess the Extent to Which You Have Adopted Digital Selling*

   To establish a baseline to work from, ask yourself:

   - To what extent am I leveraging social media and other digital channels to expand my circle of relationships with potential buyers?
   - Which of the inbound and outbound tools listed earlier in this chapter are my company and I using today?
   - What tools am I utilizing to help do the selling in between meetings or conversations with my customers?

2. *Think About What Steps You Already Feel Compelled to Take*

   The rest of this book is chock-full of highly actionable suggestions for how to embrace and master digital selling. But even before we go any further, ask yourself:

   - What additional platforms or tools do I already know I want to better leverage?
   - What actions could I take this week to make progress on one or more of these?
   - Which competencies mentioned in this chapter should I make time to explore and research further?

3. *Register for Access to All the Tools, Templates, and Minicourses*

   Throughout this book I'll be talking about and referencing a wide variety of resources I've created to help you get the most out of every chapter. It is my privilege to share all of these with you at no charge! Just go to www.salesexcellence.com/handbook to get started.

Enjoy!

CHAPTER 2

Engaging Customers Early in Their Digital Buying Process

The opening of my first book, *Think Like Your Customer* (McGraw Hill 2005), featured a short story that has since been told in over 1,000 sales training workshops and keynote speeches all over the world. Whether you've heard it before or not, the main takeaway from this story is worth remembering and living by. If we are to thrive in this rapidly changing digital marketplace, this truth applies now more than ever.

As a kid I was blessed to spend a lot of time going fishing with my dad. Many of those trips were mini-adventures filled with unexpected challenges and a variety of hilarious mishaps that I will never forget. I learned many life lessons through those years. But the most valuable was a certain little gem that my dad taught me when I would get frustrated watching him catch fish in almost any situation while I could seldom catch a thing. His best advice on fishing was simply this: "If you want to catch a fish, you have to think like a fish!"

At first, I couldn't understand how what I *thought* would have any impact whatsoever on my ability to catch a fish. My only question was, "What do I need to *do* to get a bass to bite this lure or a trout to take this fly?"

Over time I started to understand what my dad was really trying to teach me. What he meant was this: "If you want to catch a fish, you have to think *about* what fish think *about*." Once I grasped that, everything changed!

As I internalized that mindset, I learned to think about things like water levels, water clarity, water temperature, vegetation, food sources, feeding cycles, and a host of other factors. Carefully evaluating those variables is what enables an experienced fisherman to locate fish, assess the factors that are influencing their thinking and behavior, and ultimately entice them to bite—at least sometimes.

Eventually, I began to realize that my own thinking was often the primary determining factor in my success or failure in pretty much everything in life, not just fishing! This "think like a fish" approach has been the hallmark of my business career and represents the most important truth anyone could ever learn about sales, marketing, or entrepreneurship.

Put simply . . .

If you want to better attract, serve, and retain customers, you have to learn to think about what customers think about. Commit to studying and internalizing the psychology of how and why customers buy.

Asking how to catch a fish is the wrong question. What we need to know is what would cause a fish to bite or not bite in the first place. Likewise, asking how to make a sale is the wrong question. What we really need to understand is what would cause a customer to buy and how has the advent of so many new technologies changed the manner in which they do so.

How Customers Think When They Buy

For many years I have a used a diagram in my workshops I call the Customer Results Model as shown in Figure 2.1. It's a visual illustration that helps illuminate how customers think as they make buying decisions. This idea has become the foundation for nearly all of the many training programs that I've developed over the years. It's simple, which is what makes it so useful. But it has the potential to dramatically change the way we think, the way we communicate with clients, and the way we sell, especially in today's digital-first marketplace.

The way I define it, a buying process begins when a customer recognizes some dissatisfaction with their current state. This is when they realize they have some sort of need, pain, problem, or challenge that is significant enough to do something about. I call this moment of recognition *Point A* as shown in Figure 2.1. Until a customer arrives at this place, they probably won't buy anything. And they shouldn't! But if the need or the pain they recognize and the consequences of remaining at Point A are significant enough, a potential sales opportunity is born.

Figure 2.1   Customer Results Model

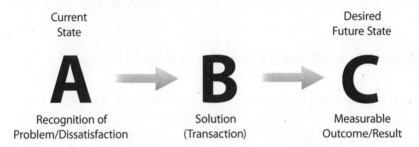

If we think we can provide some kind of a product or service solution that would help the prospective customer, our goal as a seller becomes moving them from Point A to a place we will call *Point B*, where some sort of transaction takes place. We provide a *solution* in exchange for money. A sale is made!

At Point B, we could easily conclude that we are done! We book the order, earn some commission, and move on to the next opportunity. But for the customer, Point B is just the beginning. Now they have to go out and use whatever we sold them with the hope of arriving at what we'll call *Point C*, or their desired future state.

One of the most challenging lessons in sales and marketing is recognizing that . . .

> **Nobody really wants to buy whatever solution you sell at Point B. What they want is to *use* what you sell to get the outcomes and results they want to achieve at Point C.**

For example, pharmaceutical companies don't want laboratory instruments. What they want is the ability to more quickly identify and develop compounds to be used in new drugs to improve people's health and save lives. Likewise, your customers don't want unified communication systems. What they want is a fully connected workforce that is productive enough to maintain high levels of customer satisfaction—which ensures customer retention—while working from any home or office in the world.

Most of what is sold in this world is not an end unto itself; more often it's a means to an end. Our customers buy some sort of product or services solution to obtain their desired outcome. While we might sell a solution, what our customer actually buys is a result! This means that we have to move beyond just selling solutions. We have to learn how to sell outcomes and results!

Aligning with How Customers Buy

Now, chronologically—and of course alphabetically—the three letters used in this diagram appear A, B, and then C. But if we look more closely at the way customers think when they buy, we see that their thinking process is more often A, then C, and then back to B.

Once your customers recognize their dissatisfaction at A, they usually start imagining and visualizing what life might be like if they could get to C. Assuming that desired future state is compelling enough, they'll probably start thinking about how to get there. This might include making an investment at B in some vehicle that would get them from where they are to where they want to go, as shown in Figure 2.2.

Figure 2.2   Customer Results Model Applied

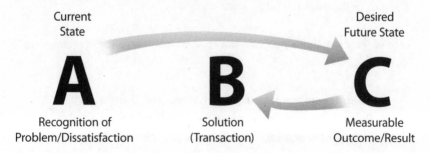

Current State		Desired Future State
A	**B**	**C**
Recognition of Problem/Dissatisfaction	Solution (Transaction)	Measurable Outcome/Result

For many years, I've taught this model as a highly effective format for real-time selling—where you can engage your client in a live conversation. You can start by asking questions to prompt the customer to talk about their current state problem, pain, need, issue, or some situation they are dissatisfied with. Then, you can help them assess the consequences of their current state (A). Help them determine what that situation is costing them using the units of measure that matter most to them, such as dollars spent, hours wasted, customers lost, and so on.

Once the client has acknowledged their problem or dissatisfaction, you can then lead the conversation to explore their desired future state. As you do this, make sure to quantify the value of the results they want to achieve using units of measure related to their desired outcomes, such as increasing gross revenue, accelerating the time to full productivity for new hires, improving customer renewal rates, and so forth. The more you can crystallize their C, and the more you can define the measurable return, the better you can craft an ideal solution and justify whatever investment is required at B.

This exact same model, which is incredibly effective for real-time selling, is the perfect tool to guide our efforts for creating the content and assets we can use for asynchronous digital selling as well. It can be used by salespeople in their outbound emails as well as by marketeers to create website copy, social media content, marketing collateral, and so on.

So much of what is published in social media and blog posts or made into videos for company websites is all about B. It's all about our company and what we offer. But it doesn't have to be that way! We can use social posts, published articles, YouTube videos, or really any medium to pose questions and engage readers and viewers in e-conversations about *their* current state (A) and desired future state (C). Over these next few chapters, we're going to learn how to use this more outcome-oriented approach as we help our clients work through the decisions involved in their buying process even when selling asynchronously.

The Big Shift and the Quantum Leap

This Customer Results Model is designed to cause two specific epiphanies in the evolution of every salesperson, marketer, or business owner who sees it. The first of these I call the *big shift*.

> **The big shift occurs when we recognize our responsibility
> is not just presenting and promoting our product but
> helping our customers make smart decisions as they
> work through the steps of their buying process.**

This is huge! Even for those of us who've been around long enough to know better, it's just too easy to get in a hurry, or maybe get a little lazy, and forget to diagnose our customer's problem before we prescribe a solution. We focus on "making the sale" and lose sight of the steps the customer has to take and the various decisions they have to make before they *can* buy. What we need to do is identify the questions in the customer's mind and provide the answers to those questions so they can make good decisions every step of the way.

Once we've made the big shift and start to focus less on selling and more on facilitating our customer's buying process, the next major breakthrough for most of us is what I refer to as the *quantum leap* . . .

> **The quantum leap happens when we embrace the fact
> that today we often need to empower customers to work
> through buying decisions entirely asynchronously.**

Ouch! Many of us don't want to hear that. That's why I call this the quantum leap. We don't want to give up the perceived control we have in real-time, synchronous selling. But that control we think we have is a false perception. We lost that control the instant one of our competitors put up a series of YouTube videos to answer customer questions that used to require a face-to-face meeting. Today's buyers are drawing conclusions and making decisions without us because they can!

Your would-be customers may take the time to peruse your website. They may look at your LinkedIn profile. They might even watch a couple of your videos on YouTube. But if they aren't impressed by what they see, they probably won't call you or respond to your calls and emails to them. Therefore, the digital assets you post or send have to be created to do at least some of the selling for you. They at least have to be good enough to sell the right to have a conversation!

Is it possible to empower your customers to make better decisions at each stage of their buying process using only the written word, graphics, audio, or video? Absolutely! The question is whether we *will* or not. Unfortunately, it doesn't matter whether we *want* to do it. If we are to remain competitive, we basically don't have a choice! If we don't do it, somebody else will!

How Buyer/Seller Engagement Has Changed

Prior to the arrival of the World Wide Web, most buyers had no choice but to meet or get on the phone with a seller if they needed help solving a problem. Information about the products and services buyers had an interest in came in the form of a printed catalog, a brochure, or a conversation with a person who could provide those products and services.

Throughout the late 1990s and early 2000s, nearly every company tried to push as much information about themselves and their offerings to the web as possible. Through the years resources like online forums, blogs, YouTube, and a variety of social media platforms made it possible for buyers to learn about companies or even individual sellers from their colleagues, industry experts, and independent researchers. During the most recent decade, information and opinions from third-party sources have become absolutely ubiquitous.

Today, consumers and even B2B buyers often gather more information about the products and services available to them from these third-party sources—Google reviews, Yelp, and research firms like Gartner—than from the companies that sell the products themselves. It's quite sobering when you realize that today's customer often puts more credence in what people on the internet say about you than what you say about yourself!

All of this has led us to a place where the first conversation buyers have with an actual salesperson often comes much later in their buying process than ever before. Buyers frequently recognize their dissatisfaction with their current state and begin their buying journey based on what they read, watch, and listen to online. The typical point of buyer and seller engagement has changed drastically over the years, as illustrated in Figure 2.3.

Figure 2.3   First Point of Customer Engagement

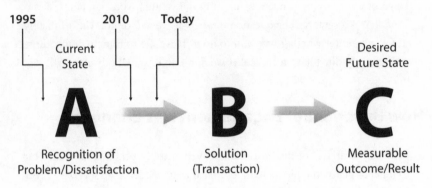

Today, your customers can simply go to their favorite search engine and start typing in the problem they are having or the business outcome they want to achieve. They can go on YouTube and see other people just like themselves talking about how they solved the same problem or achieved the same desired outcome. Maybe they will join an online forum of their peers, such as a LinkedIn group or a public Slack (www.slack.com) channel, to ask how other people have addressed the issues they face. The point is they no longer need *you* to provide the information required to make buying decisions. Oftentimes, they decide what they need and want first, and then they call you and three other providers to see who has the best price.

A number of years ago, Brent Adamson, who was the principal executive advisor at CEB at the time, released the findings of a widely referenced study that showed that, on average, a B2B buyer was 57 percent of the way through their buying process before they personally engaged a salesperson.[1] More recent studies state that the point of engagement is now 60 percent or even 70 percent of the way through the process.

These statistics have been misinterpreted by many to mean that we shouldn't bother trying to engage clients earlier in their process. The thinking is: They don't want to hear from us. Let's just focus our selling efforts on that last 30 or 40 percent of the process after the prospect calls us or fills out a request-for-information form on our website. I totally disagree!

The best time to engage your target clients is before a project even exists! You want to be the one who helps your client recognize their dissatisfaction and paints the picture of the ideal Point C you can help them achieve.

You want to help shape perception and earn preference long before a need becomes a deal. Otherwise, you relegate yourself to being just another "bidder."

Let's say you are an outside account executive with a deck of 25 target accounts. If the first time you have any personal contact with the key buyers and influencers in one of these accounts is when they are 60+ percent of the way through a buying process, you've probably already lost the deal. Those of us who are hunters can't afford to wait around for our target prospects to contact us! In that kind of sales environment, a proactive outbound approach is imperative! But your initial outreach doesn't necessarily have to be a cold telephone call to request a one-hour meeting. Today, we usually have to get a little more creative than that.

Empowering Customers Throughout Their Buying Process

In his book *The Ultimate Sales Machine* (Portfolio 2007), author Chet Holmes offered a diagram that is quite eye-opening for just about everyone involved in sales and marketing. Chet says he drew these conclusions about the composition of a typical market based on personal observations and regularly polling the audiences that he spoke to.

Even though the exact percentages he used are not scientifically validated, the truth that is revealed—and that you and I can apply—is just as powerful as if it were based on an extensive study. It's so good that dozens of other authors have since copyrighted it, published it, and called it their own. Here's my version based on Chet's idea, shown in Figure 2.4.

Only about 3 percent of the people or companies in a typical market are actually ready to buy something at any given time.[2] These "Top 3 percent" are in *buying mode* and are the ones who typically respond to advertising and outbound sales prospecting. If we happen to put something in front of them at the right time, they are likely to visit our website and submit a request for information. Maybe they'll even respond to an outbound email marketing campaign or telephone call.

Beyond those who are currently in buying mode, there is another 7 percent or so who are "open to explore." In years past, these "Open 7 percent" would often agree to a telephone conversation if we proposed one.

Figure 2.4   Pyramid of Awareness

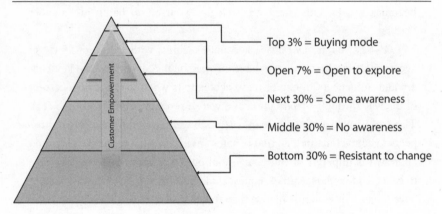

Top 3% = Buying mode

Open 7% = Open to explore

Next 30% = Some awareness

Middle 30% = No awareness

Bottom 30% = Resistant to change

But because of how digital buying has evolved, these "lookers" now often prefer to attend the occasional webinar (with their camera off, of course) or poke around various websites and YouTube channels at their leisure. Maybe they'll even exchange their phone number for the right to download an article or a white paper once in a while. But unless that white paper is written specifically to resonate with their dissatisfaction with A or clearly lays out the payback available at C, they frequently won't even pick up the phone when we call to follow up.

In terms of practical application, companies or individuals who are willing to do the work involved in outbound prospecting can make a first pass on a target list of prospects with email or telephone campaigns. That is probably the quickest way to reveal those in the Top 3 percent and the Open 7 percent who are willing to have a sales conversation. Some are!

Here's my belief . . .

> **It's not as if outbound selling motions don't work anymore. It's the nature of our approach and the substance of what we attempt to communicate *with* our outbound efforts that needs an extreme makeover!**

We'll talk about this much more extensively in Chapter 7.

The "Next 30 percent" have some awareness of their own need for help at some point. They might already know we exist and may even be starting to sense a bit of dissatisfaction with their current state, but not enough to really explore. Then comes the "Middle 30 percent" that have no awareness of their own need for help yet. And last, we have the "Bottom 30 percent" who are not only unaware they might ever need what we have to provide, but are opposed to even thinking about it. Perhaps they just made an investment in something similar to what we offer and can't imagine ever being in a different situation. Maybe their brother-in-law works for our competitor. Or maybe they're just grumpy! Who knows?

I remember the days when the Top 3 percent were actively ringing our telephone to get answers to their questions. The Open 7 percent were happy to take our phone calls or even book a meeting if we happened to be in their area. Even the Next 30 percent would occasionally attend an introductory seminar if it was close enough to their office and we had free Starbucks coffee and Cinnabon rolls. Obviously, things are a little different now.

The conventional "numbers game" approach to selling has always been about finding and selling to the Top 3 percent who are buying now and spending almost all of our time and effort there. That strategy was effective back when buyers had a greater need for a seller's help in terms of education and information. Now, they have the ability to locate, research, and draw conclusions about us and other potential suppliers long before we ever know they exist!

Therefore . . .

Focusing on finding and selling only to the Top 3 percent is a flawed strategy today because by the time they arrive there, customers already have a strong preference for the company that *helped* them get there digitally. If it's not us, our odds of winning drop off dramatically.

The real opportunity lies in engaging with your prospective customers regardless of what level they occupy and empowering them to move up through the pyramid of awareness. You'll want to literally lead them all the way into the Top 3 percent when the time is right. The upward arrow in Figure 2.4 represents the building of e-relationships that empower your prospects to become potential customers. Once empowered, future customers start to feel as if they know you and already have a strong preference for doing business with you before they ever get to the top of the pyramid. Now let's talk about how to do that.

Engaging in the Early Stages with Insight

For a visual illustration of what *customer empowerment* looks like in action, let's turn that pyramid on its side and overlay it onto my Customer Results Model. This shows how awareness typically progresses as the customer moves from Point A to Point B. See Figure 2.5.

Figure 2.5   Engaging Earlier in Your Customer's Buying Process

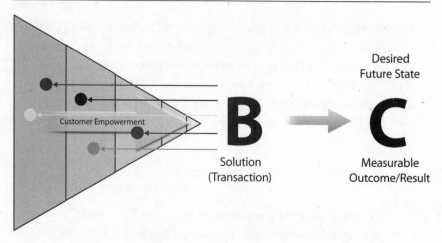

Traditional advertising and cold-call prospecting are most effective with the Top 3 percent who are buying now and the Open 7 percent who might consider looking.

This means . . .

**Roughly 90 percent of our market is unlikely to
respond to advertising and cold-calling, so we have
to *reach back* into the earlier stages of their buying
process and engage them in a different way.**

People who aren't in the upper 10 percent (the Top 3 percent plus Open 7 percent) that are currently buying or looking typically won't respond to an advertisement that's all about us and the products and services we have for sale (our B). If we want to connect with them, we have to offer them something they find value in reading or watching that talks about their A or their C. We need to provide digital assets that are relevant and helpful to them, wherever they are in the pyramid. For those in the lower 90 percent, we can't just throw them another ad. We need to offer *insight.*

Insight is a piece of information that brings about a new way of looking at something. It causes introspection. It enables the reader to make a new deduction or arrive at a different conclusion. Insight manifests itself as a sudden understanding of how to solve a difficult problem or obtain a desired result. Insight can produce an *epiphany* or a *eureka moment.* I like to call these *aha* moments or even *uh-oh* moments. The intent is to cause the reader to think, "Wow, I never thought about it like that before."

The basic strategy for much of advertising is to make it easy for people to find us when they are ready to buy. Digital selling using insight, on the other hand, helps people *get ready* to buy by providing knowledge, guidance, and information that changes their perception of:

- Their dissatisfaction of the current state (A)
- The consequences of remaining at A
- The possibilities available at their desired future state (C)
- The payback or return when they reach C
- Why they should take action now
- Why we are the ideal partner to help them

Those who master digital selling will use insight to help customers draw favorable conclusions and make smart decisions at every point in their buying process.

When delivered well, insight provides context for interpreting new data, real-world examples, suggestions for practical application, and proven best practices. Insight changes hearts and minds. Insight literally generates demand! Empowering customers with insight that moves them upward through the pyramid toward that Top 3 percent is the way we create a preference for doing business with us once they get there.

People tend to rely more heavily on information they gather early in their discovery process. Psychologists call this *anchor bias*. The person or company that brings new insight to the buying process—and creates those aha moments when buyers are in their exploratory stages—usually becomes the point of reference by which all other sources of information are compared later on.

When selling in real time, of course, insight can be shared verbally. In my opinion, *this* is still the ideal approach *if* and when you can get an appointment with your buyer for a synchronous conversation. In an early-stage live discussion, my goal is always to spark conversation and get my customer talking by asking them diagnostic questions they wouldn't think to ask themselves. If you can get your customer to rub their chin and say, "Hmmm. That's a good question," then you know you've got them thinking differently than they were before you came along.

Asking questions to seek understanding about their current state and desired future state not only helps us better select and position the right solution, but it literally causes your customers to see things differently and arrive at new conclusions. You also earn trust and rapport along the way. Hearing their responses in real time and then asking good follow-up questions that lead them to your way of thinking is truly selling at its finest. Honestly, I wish *all* selling could be synchronous selling! That's just not always possible today.

When it comes to digital selling in an asynchronous fashion, insight can be shared in a wide variety of formats:

- Website or landing page copy

- Videos on websites, social platforms, or YouTube

- Downloadable assets like white papers, studies, or a "free guide" of some sort

- Social media posts, either organic or paid

- Comments you leave on other people's posts

- Articles, books, and ebooks

- Blog posts, either on your own blog or as a guest on someone else's

- Podcasts, either your own or as a guest on someone else's

- Online text-based, live-audio, and live-video discussion forums

- Digital advertorials and other paid or bartered digital content placement

To illustrate how to use insight in one or more of these ways, let's look at a few different examples of how you could share some of your knowledge and experience in the form of an article entitled "5 Ways Manufacturers Are Hemorrhaging Money by Using Obsolete _____ Systems." Fill in the blank or reword this sample title to make it relevant to your market and the solutions you provide.

Posting a piece like this as a blog or an article on LinkedIn creates a powerful digital asset for "inbound" selling that could appeal to just about everyone. When designed well, it can help us earn credibility and trust with those in the upper 10 percent as well as trigger those in the lower 90 percent to want to explore things further and move upward through the pyramid stack.

Once you have an asset like this, you can also send this article as an attachment or a hyperlink in an email or LinkedIn message as part of your outbound strategy. You could even shoot a video delivering the same insight and leverage that on YouTube and then send the link within an email. In the coming chapters, I'll offer a wide variety of ways to deliver your insight both inbound and outbound. But the secret is not in the delivery mechanism. The key is the intent and the substance of your article or video content itself!

Please note: This particular example is *not* an article on the technical details of your new product or all the whiz-bang functions of your latest technology. It's also not a side-by-side "shoot-out" comparison showing how you annihilate your top three major competitors. That kind of information has its place, especially for the Top 3 percent and the Open 7 percent. We need those digital assets, too! But the lower 90 percent of the market probably won't respond to that yet. Choosing who to buy from just isn't relevant if your buyer hasn't yet concluded they need to explore buying anything in the first place.

Whenever possible, focus on creating separate marketing and outreach campaigns for those people and companies you believe are currently in the upper 10 percent versus the lower 90 percent. Today, there are tools that can help you determine which ones are which using "intent data," which we'll talk about later. Initiate different kinds of e-conversations for each group. Do specific outcome-oriented marketing about solutions that appeal to the upper 10 percent, and deliver well-crafted insight that influences the perceptions of the lower 90 percent.

Frankly, the 90 percent who aren't buying or looking right now don't want to be sold to. They simply won't tolerate being inundated by a never-ending barrage of ads and pitches. They will tune you out, block your phone number, mark you as spam, or promptly unfollow. But even the Bottom 30 percent, who are often totally annoyed by ads and prospecting outreach, see value in insight if it's of benefit to them in their current situation.

What if you wrote an article or shot a video called, "How to Maximize Your Return on Investment in _____?" (Fill in the blank with whatever you sell.) Even the companies who just bought your competitor's product might be interested in reading that! When they do, you earn credibility and are seen as an expert in return on investment, not just a guy schlepping another product. They might call you in as a consultant to help them with a broader initiative or to bail them out if their implementation goes awry. Or maybe they'll reach out to you when they move on to a different company nine months later.

If you serve brick-and-mortar retailers, for example, how about writing a series of LinkedIn posts to be released every Tuesday morning called "6 Colossal Mistakes Today's Retailers Cannot Afford to Make"? Each of the six installments should be written to cause the reader to experience one of those aha moments and walk away thinking or doing something different than they were before they read it. Always share your insight with the intent of altering your reader's beliefs and perceptions.

YouTube is probably the best and most underutilized platform for sharing insights with your market in an informative and engaging way while building familiarity and rapport at the same time. Sharing one or more new nuggets of insight on YouTube every week has been the starting point for thousands of successful "YouTubers" as well as companies who regularly "feed" their subscribers and empower them to become paying customers when the time is right.

Make sure to let the reader or the viewer know to tune in the following week for the next episode. Good old-fashioned curiosity could cause some of them to reach out to you right now because they don't want to wait six weeks to hear all of your helpful suggestions.

Here are a few more examples of possible titles for digital assets that could completely change the e-conversations you are having with your future customers. As you read, think about which words you would change to make these relevant to your industry. Maybe even write a few headlines or titles of your own:

5 Risks You Run by Not Moving Your Mission-Critical Applications to the Cloud

6 Incredibly Powerful Ways to Improve Customer Service and Minimize Churn

Assessing the Consequences and Costs of Not Embracing 5G Wireless

3 Major Pitfalls to Avoid When Implementing a New Payroll System

7 Little-Known Ways to Quantify Your Return on Investment in Sales Training

4 Reasons Why Do-It-Yourself Property Management Could Cost You Big Money

It's crucial here not to allow an article like this to become just a poorly disguised product pitch or stealth brochure. If you're going to add insight, make it interesting, objective, and focused on solving problems and achieving results. If the only advice or recommendation you offer is "you need to buy my product," you'll squander all the credibility and authority you worked so hard to establish.

I bet you've noticed that almost all of these sample topics begin with a number and promise multiple fresh insights right in the title. Most people cannot resist the promise of four, or five, or six new ideas that relate to some business outcome that matters to them. They figure, "Surely one of these suggestions has to be applicable in my situation." Professional head-line writers almost always use the numeral at the beginning instead of spelling out the number.

You can give away multiple select tips in one downloadable document or break them into pieces. Sharing one tip at a time daily or weekly on social media can be a very effective way to keep your audience coming back for more. Or you can offer people a collection of insights in exchange for their contact information or for registering for your upcoming free online mas-terclass. I'll have a ton of additional ideas for how to use these kinds of assets coming your way throughout the rest of the book.

Sharing Your Knowledge and Insight with Your Market

Some who are reading this are thinking, "Wait a minute. I'm not going to give away all my trade secrets and all my advice on the internet for free! That's what people pay me for! One of my competitors might read it, and I would be out of business!" If that's you, you wouldn't be the first person to think that. That fear is surely one of the main reasons so many people never really step into using insights to engage with prospective customers early in their buying process.

But the most effective marketeers today, the voices that others want to follow, the "influencers" in this world that shape market perception, *are* influ-ential because they freely share their throughts and opinions with everyone. When they do, the people who follow them and value their knowledge and expertise are more than happy to buy whatever they offer or recommend.

The best example I can give you of the power of selling through sharing insights is the very book you are holding in your hands. As you can see, I am giving away everything I have learned through a lifetime in the selling profession basically free of charge. If you knew how few pennies an author earns on each book sold, you'd agree that this is not exactly a high-profit endeavor. But here's what I can tell you.

When *Think Like Your Customer* was released in the fall of 2004, my business and my career went from "really good" to "beyond my wildest dreams." When that book appeared on the shelves of bookstores around the world, was displayed right next to the cash register at hundreds of FedEx

Kinko's stores (now FedEx Office), and became a category bestseller on Amazon.com, my whole life changed!

Now let's be clear: I'm not Stephen King or J. K. Rowling. But within a few months, I had senior executives at companies all over the world calling my phone number and asking me to train their global sales teams and speak at their annual sales conferences. Despite the fact that I put every good idea I had into that book, somehow people still wanted more. I had just shared everything I knew in exchange for less than a buck-a-copy in royalties. But the business engagements that flowed from that exposure have paid the bills quite nicely for nearly 20 years.

If you're not quite ready to publish your first book yet, start with one well-crafted post on LinkedIn! Maybe cowrite an article with one of your product engineers that speaks to how your solutions can be used to solve a particular business problem that many of your customers face.

Ask your best client to provide a testimonial and turn it into a short story that you can publish. Maybe even record a video of a client talking about how you've helped them improve their business performance and post that video on YouTube. Take what you know and share it with the world free of charge! I assure you that the people who like what they see are going to want to hear more.

Take the case of a gentleman I know named Allyn Hane, as an example. He launched a YouTube channel called "The Lawn Care Nut" about 10 years ago and started posting a weekly video with tips about his passion for cultivating a fabulous lawn. When he realized that his little audience had become a viable marketplace, he decided to launch his own line of lawn care products that he could recommend on his show.

At the time of this writing, Allyn has more than 493,000 subscribers, which is about double what he had just 18 months ago. Lots of people sell lawn care products. Not all that many have hundreds of thousands of people watching a new video episode every week on exactly how they can use those products to achieve the amazing lawn they've always dreamed of.

Are you ready to take me up on the challenge? Learn to engage your prospective customers at every stage of their buying process by delivering every morsel of knowledge and insight you can produce through a variety of communication channels. Over the next several chapters I'm going to show you how to become a trusted resource for your prospective customers, not just another person "selling" something.

Putting These Ideas into Practice

Before we proceed, may I suggest taking the following steps to ensure that you are fully leveraging the ideas presented here:

1. *Create a Problems and Results Inventory*

   Literally make a list of problems you and your company can help customers solve at Point A and the results you can help your customers achieve at Point C. Try to list at least 12 of each. The first 3 or 4 will come quickly. But to get to 8 or 10 or 12 you'll have to get more creative. The goal is to equip you with talking points and a basis for asking good questions that reveal opportunities to help your customer. If you'd like a worksheet to help with this process, download the Problems and Results Inventory worksheet at: http://www.salesexcellence.com/handbook.

2. *Title at Least Three Articles or Videos*

   Brainstorm about what you could create that would provide insights that your customer needs at various levels within the pyramid of awareness.

3. *Write or Record Something for at Least One of Those Titles*

   It doesn't have to be all you. Leverage the expertise of others on your team to produce something that helps your customer recognize a current state need or a desired future state goal or objective.

4. *Post or Share Your New Digital Asset*

   You can post your new article on a blog or on LinkedIn. You can place your new video on YouTube or on your website. Or maybe just write a simple post on LinkedIn about the problems you solve and the results you can deliver. Don't expect your very first try to be a masterpiece. And don't wait until you've got all the graphic design just right.

I've learned that . . .

> **Perfectionism is a form of procrastination usually driven by fear of what other people are going to think. Get past that! Do something *imperfect* with these ideas today.**

CHAPTER 3

Mastering Digital Selling and Content Development

Irecently read an article on modern-day selling that did a really nice job of showcasing a variety of the latest sales enablement tools. It offered the reader some good advice on embracing digital automation systems and even a nice list of ways to make use of the latest technologies to attract prospects and reach out to new clients.

The last bullet on the list of suggestions was simply, "Post on LinkedIn Every Day." As you might imagine, I wholeheartedly concur. But I couldn't help but think that advice sounded a bit vague. That suggestion seemed kind of like telling someone, "Make one phone call every day!" Or maybe, "Make 20 phone calls every day!" That's not *bad* advice, by any means. But if you did decide to make one phone call a day (or 20), you might also find yourself asking:

- Who should I call?
- Where can I reach them?
- When should I call them?
- Why would I be calling in the first place? (What would be the objective?)
- What would I want to say, ask, or communicate to them?
- If it went well, what should I ask the customer to do next?
- How could I help them choose to take the next logical step?

Just making a phone call might not amount to anything if you don't put some thought into questions that begin with words like *who*, *what*, *where*, *when*, *why*, and *how*.

Likewise, as you think more deeply about your overall digital selling strategy, and especially about creating the content you'll use for inbound and outbound demand generation, many of these same kinds of questions apply:

- Who do you hope will see or consume this content?

- Where should you publish it? (What is the best platform to use to deliver it?)

- When, or on what cadence, would you want to release it?

- Why would you be posting this to begin with? (What is the intended objective?)

- What should you say or try to communicate with this piece of content?

- If you capture their interest, what should you ask customers to do next?

- How could you persuade the reader or viewer to take the next logical step?

We don't call someone just to say we called someone. We also shouldn't post or publish something just to say we published something. Any and all of our efforts should be directed to accomplish a specific purpose.

We're going to explore formats and platforms as we go. But the bulk of this chapter will focus on what is actually written and/or said *within* your sales and marketing content. We're going to explore the objective of why we are posting or publishing in the first place.

We'll look closely at how customers make buying decisions. We will uncover how to influence customer perceptions as we help them draw conclusions about us, about what we offer, but also about *themselves*. We're going to apply a method to our digital selling that can be leveraged throughout all of our e-conversations with our target audience regardless of platform or medium.

The goal is not simply to get your name out there, hoping someone remembers you when they find themselves ready to buy something. The true objective of digital demand generation is to move people upward through that pyramid of awareness we discussed in Chapter 2 and empower them to arrive in the Top 3 percent with a strong preference for doing business with you.

Selling Via Content with Intent

Every bit of content that we write and record should be created to influence our prospective customers' perceptions and beliefs. As I've said previously, we need to use our website copy, our YouTube videos, and our social posts to do more than just gain "visibility" or "exposure." We're trying to literally change hearts and minds.

Through all of your digital communication with your client, the aim is to . . .

> Create and deliver *content with intent*. What do you want your reader or viewer to think differently or do differently after they consume what you've written or recorded?

The power of selling via content—especially via video—was illustrated profoundly by an inquiry we received through our website a few months ago. A new prospective client from the United Kingdom contacted us, and we scheduled a videoconference. If I hadn't been on this call myself, I never would have believed this story. But this is exactly how it went.

Once we joined the conference and exchanged pleasantries, the gentleman started by saying:

"It's really great to meet you in person, Bill! We found your company listed as one of the Top 20 Online Sales Training Companies in *Selling Power* magazine. We've been to your website and looked at the various programs you offer. We've also watched your videos on YouTube. We'd like to talk about having you work with us on a training project if you can fit us in."

I was curious, so I asked, "Which video did you watch?"

"We watched all of them," he replied.

"All of them?" I questioned.

"Well, all of them we could find, anyway. We especially liked the one where you contrasted your method for blending short micro-learning challenges with live-video accountability sessions as compared to the more traditional online e-learning courses, which our guys have become bored with."

"Well, I'm glad that resonated with you!"

He said, "We sent a few of the videos around to our sales leaders, and they feel like your approach and some of the topics you offer would be a great fit for us. We also noticed you've worked with quite a few companies in the life sciences industry."

"Yes, we sure have."

He continued, "My boss was impressed with the clip of the British executive who talked about how you customized your course just for his company and the markets they sell to. We weren't sure we'd be able to get this program kicked off until our next fiscal year, but then we saw one of your videos on LinkedIn where you talked about your ability to custom-tailor your programs so you can start delivering training within three to four weeks. Is that right?

"Yes, sir!" I reassured him.

"So, we thought, 'Let's see if we can get this kicked off before we get too far into our fourth quarter.'"

"I think that's definitely possible," I said.

He went on to say, "Our general manager also liked the video where you talked about the key metrics you use to measure the success of a training program. He's been telling us that if we spend money developing this team, we'd better be able to show a return on the investment. So that video helped a lot!"

I was blown away! Talk about being far down the buying path! This couldn't have been a more textbook example of exactly why we created all those videos in the first place! The client and his colleagues were able to answer so many questions for themselves before we ever even spoke. They drew a variety of conclusions and even alleviated many of their own fears by looking at online endorsements and testimonials.

Let's quickly recap a few of the conclusions that he and his colleagues were able to draw as a result of what they could read and watch online:

1. We're a reputable company with a global reach.

2. We have a lot of experience training salespeople in his industry.

3. We can help their team in the specific areas in which they feel they need the most help.

4. We can quickly custom tailor the program to align with their go-to-market strategy.

5. We've got a lot of happy clients, so maybe they would end up being happy too!

6. They could get started sooner than they realized.

7. They would be able to track their results and quantify their return on investment.

By sharing links to specific videos with various internal stakeholders, they were even able to build consensus with enough people to get the support they needed to move forward with the project. That's amazing! The great news for all of us is that this kind of digital selling is not rocket science. Anybody who's willing to learn can and should be doing this constantly and *intentionally.*

What if you put some serious thought into the kinds of things that your buyers might need to know so they could draw conclusions and make some important decisions before they ever speak with you? What would you want your clients to conclude about you and what you offer? If you decided to create just one new digital asset like this, what would you want it to persuade your prospects to think or do?

If we knew the answers to these questions, we could create content that was specifically designed to provide the information our prospects need to arrive at *our* preferred conclusions. We don't need to produce more content just so we can post "something" on LinkedIn every day. Digital content should be used to actually sell!

Let's remember this . . .

The quantity and frequency of publishing digital selling assets definitely matters—as does how you choose to deliver them. But what matters more is the way you make people think and feel after they read or watch them.

Digital content can educate, stimulate, motivate, alleviate fears, mitigate perceived risks, and even overcome objections when it's done right. I call it *digital salesmanship.* This is the future!

Once we create digital assets that are designed to change customer thinking and behavior, we can use them for inbound demand generation *and* outbound prospecting. When we use these kinds of tools in our outreach, we not only increase the likelihood of landing a meeting, but we also influence perception and challenge the thinking of anyone who chooses to look at them whether they are ready to meet with us or not.

Two Big Decisions Buyers Have to Make

Any significant buying process boils down to two big decisions that are based on the buyer answering two major questions:

1. **The Action Decision:** Do we really need to buy something now?
2. **The Choice Decision:** Who should we buy from?

That first question, which enables the customer to make a good action decision, actually includes three operative words. Those three words are *really*, *buy*, and *now*.

If your prospective customer doesn't *really* have to buy something, maybe they will just put it off for a while. Perhaps they can even get by without it forever. Few companies spend significant amounts of money on things that aren't tied to solving a particular business problem or achieving a specific measurable result. Corporate investments now require more documentation, justification, and "hoop jumping" than ever. Your customer will probably never do all of that if they don't have to. And there's always something else for your customer to spend their money on if they don't *really* have to spend it with you.

The second word that is pivotal in that question is *buy*. Customers might ask themselves, "Do we need to *buy* something? Or can we just use what we already have and figure out a way to make it work?" Or perhaps a team of people will look at each other and ask, "Can we come up with a way to build this or do it ourselves?" Sometimes there are alternate courses of action a company could take to achieve their desired results short of making a new purchase or an investment with you.

The third key word is *now*. This, of course, speaks to urgency. I've found that if a company can delay or postpone an investment and there is no negative consequence to doing so, oftentimes that's exactly what they will do. Haven't we all met plenty of clients who made all the decisions necessary to buy except that last decision to move forward *now*? How many times have you heard your customer say, "We decided to put this on the 'back burner' for now?" Ugh!

So, to complete their action decision, buyers will have to come to these conclusions:

- We *really* need this. It's not just a nice-to-have. It's a must-have.

- We need to *buy* this as opposed to trying to make it or do it ourselves.

- We need this *now*. We can't afford to wait or put this off any longer.

Assuming all of those things are true, then the second big decision, the choice decision, is this: "Who should we buy from?" I always like to point out that if a buyer never ends up making the action decision, the choice decision is irrelevant. That doesn't always mean they finalize their action decision before they ever start to consider choice. But selecting a choice and then never taking any action still results in no purchase.

Unfortunately, sometimes . . .

> **We go to such great lengths trying to convince a customer that we are their best *choice* that we totally forget that the real sale to be made is helping them decide whether they need to take *action* and buy.**

In fact, the best way to become your customer's *choice* is to help them make the action decision that is best for them. If they move forward, you are in the coveted position of being an advisor, not just a salesperson. Sometimes, sadly, it means they don't end up buying anything after all.

Action Drivers and Choice Drivers

Now, we're going one layer deeper into customer psychology by exploring the various factors that go into supporting those two big buying decisions

. that customers have to make. These factors represent the various conclusions that have to be drawn as your customer contemplates those two big decisions. I call these factors *action drivers* and *choice drivers*. Stay with me through this discussion because once this concept clicks for you, it will completely change the way you sell, whether digital or otherwise.

There are a number of different conclusions that customers have to draw to support their decision to take action and buy. It's not only a cerebral exercise—there are real constraints that have to be taken into consideration such as timing, availability of funds, internal support, and approvals. Likewise, there are several things they might have to conclude before they feel like they're prepared to make a choice of who to buy *from*. Let's look at both of these sets of factors separately.

Action Drivers

There are eight action drivers in the list that follows, coupled with the associated conclusion that your customer would have to reach for each one before they'd be ready to buy. Keep in mind that a *no* on any one of these factors can cause a delay in moving forward or derail a deal entirely.

As you read through each of these, imagine yourself being the buyer. And remember that as the solutions that we provide become larger and more complex, more people on the customer's side have to be involved in the decision and agree on the answers to these questions. Think about the various people that might need to be involved in this decision process for the kinds of solutions you sell.

Before your customers could take action and buy, they would have to concretely, or at least loosely, conclude:

1. **Motive:** We have a compelling vision of our desired future state (Point C).

2. **Consequences:** We cannot afford to stay where we are today (Point A).

3. **Urgency:** We recognize the urgency to take action on this *now*.

4. **Priority:** This endeavor is of the upmost priority to us at this time.

5. **Consensus:** We all agree on the action and the direction we need to take.

6. **Resources:** We are willing and able to invest the money, time, and manpower required to get this done.

7. **Payback/Return:** We are convinced the payback or return on the completed project is worth the investment.

8. **Risks:** We are willing to accept the risks of taking action now.

Here's my challenge to you: Think about what you can provide in writing, images, audio, or video that would help your customers draw these conclusions for themselves. Go down the list one by one and identify the format and the platform you could use to convey your knowledge and advice in each of these areas. Start to think of topics, titles, and even subject lines for emails that you could use that are pertinent to your market or industry. As we look at each one more closely, let me offer just a few suggestions for the kinds of digital selling assets you might want to leverage for each.

1. Motive

Motive refers to the root of what is really driving your customer to take action and buy. Their motive is their *why*. It might be the recognition of some significant pain at Point A or the promise of a desirable outcome at Point C. Because this is so foundational to every buying decision, content that focuses on developing the customer's *why* tends to drive the conviction to make a change of some kind as well as paint the vision of what's possible if they do. Here are just a few quick examples:

Article: *How to Solve the Problem of _____ Without Enduring _____*

Blog post: *5 Sensational Wins for Every Company Willing to Embrace _____ Now*

YouTube video: *3 Ways To Use _____ to Double Your _____ in the Next 12 Months!*

LinkedIn post with tips entitled: *What if you had a step-by-step plan to double your business this year?*

2. Consequences

Consequences are the bad things that might happen if your customer doesn't take action to buy. As I mentioned earlier, the consequences of inaction often push your customers over the line and cause them to make a commitment to change even more than their motive. You could potentially help your customers appreciate the consequences of inaction with digital assets like these:

LinkedIn article: *4 Little-Known Factors That Could Cause Your Small Business to Fail This Year*

Outbound email subject line: *How to Avoid the Fatal Trap of _____ Before It's Too Late*

Short e-book: *5 Reasons You Can't Afford to Wait to _____*

Can you see how an email subject line constructed around a specific action driver could draw your customer in and make them want to learn more? You might get higher open rates with a cryptic subject line like "Bob?" or "Did you forget?" which is designed to create raw curiosity. But readers who click through on subjects and titles that actually resonate with their concerns or their desires are far more likely to engage with the substance of your content once they do. If the reader knows what they are clicking through to, they'll be more likely to respond than those who are "baited" into opening an email with some tricky subject line that doesn't really give them any idea of what they are about to look at.

3. Urgency

Urgency refers to some compelling event or a time-bound trigger that dictates or even forces your customer to take action. I think it's important to point out that it's not the urgency to buy something that drives the timeline. It's the need to solve the problems of Point A or start experiencing the payback of Point C *within a specific time frame* that really drives urgency. Content that speaks to urgency might look something like this:

Free guide: *5 Steps You Must Take Now to Avoid Losing More of Your Best Employees*

Sequence of three emails: *3 Ways You Are Losing Profit Every Month You Put Off* _____

YouTube Live: *Why Every Small Business Needs to Take Advantage of _____ Right Now*

4. Priority

The list of things your customer needs and wants to buy will always exceed the resources they'll ever have to buy them. Consequently, companies have to prioritize how they invest their money, which means some projects will get staffed and funded and others won't. Insight that could help customers prioritize investments might take the form of one of these:

Twitter thread: *4 Reasons Why _____ Should Be a Top Priority for Every _____ Today*

LinkedIn DM: *What's More Important to You: Achieving _____? Or Avoiding _____?*

Podcast topic: *How to Prioritize IT Investments for Rapid Growth and Profitability*

5. Consensus

Consensus speaks to the need to get enough of the stakeholders that are involved in a buying decision to agree on a path forward. Lack of consensus and buy-in from key decision makers can stall a deal or kill it altogether. Suppose you could create a few digital assets that would help your customers secure the internal support they need to move forward; do you think that might be useful to them? Here are a few examples:

Article: *3 Ways a Lack of Consensus Will Tank _____ and Cripple Your _____. Here's What You Can Do About It!*

Free webinar: *How to Garner the Internal Support You Need for _____*

Free guide: *5 Steps to Gaining Consensus and Support for Your _____ Project*

6. Resources

Before your customers can buy something, they have to have the money, the time, and the manpower to not only make a purchase but also to put your product or service to use. Helping your customers find or secure the resources they need to move forward can be a critical part of your job. You can create and offer digital assets to advise them and help them along the way, including the following:

Email subject line: *5 Ways to Obtain Funding When You Don't Have a Budget for* _____

YouTube video: *How Innovative Companies Are Finding Ways to Invest in* _____

LinkedIn post: *#1 Hack for Getting Funding and Approval for* _____

7. Payback/Return

Another key factor in your customer's action decision is concluding that the payback or the return available at Point C is worth the investment required at Point B. In fact, in most cases the potential return needs to be 5, 10, or even 20 times greater than the investment to offset the risk that the return may never materialize. There are a lot of different digital assets that could be used to help your customer make this decision. Here are a couple of really good ones:

Spreadsheet template: *Business Case Calculator to Justify Your Investment in* _____

Checklist: *7 Steps to Maximize Your ROI for* _____ *Projects*

LinkedIn video: *How to Measure Return on Investment for* _____

8. Risks

Perhaps the biggest hurdle any customer has to clear as part of their buying decision is getting past the perceived risks involved in making a purchase, an investment, or a change in suppliers. Risk is something we need to talk about openly with our customers so we can understand their concerns, fears, and/or misconceptions. Until we know the risks that a buyer perceives to moving forward, we are basically powerless to help them overcome or mitigate those risks, whether they be real or imaginary. Content that helps the customer overcome perceived risks could include the following:

Research study: *Why the Risk of Switching to* _____ *Is Nothing Compared to the Risk of* _____ *(not switching)*

Weekly email sequence: *4 Ways to Mitigate Your Risk of* _____ *Without* _____ *(negative consequence)*

Twitter livestream: *How to Minimize Your Exposure to* _____ *by Investing in* _____ *Now*

* * *

I'm sure you are already formulating a ton of ideas about how you could start using digital assets to influence, persuade, and help your customers draw favorable conclusions related to making their action decision—even when you're not around. That's how you leverage technology to scale your capacity to sell!

Please note that some of these assets can be published and posted free of charge. Others could be shared in exchange for contact information to grow your email subscriber list. Some might only be shared privately with prospects in the final stages of their buying process. And yet others might be something you could turn into a marketable, low-cost product to create what I call a "starter customer." We'll discuss these uses further in Chapter 5.

Choice Drivers

It's easy to overgeneralize by saying, "Customers buy from people they know, like, and trust." We all know this is true. But this assumes that the seller has a product or service the customer needs, that it can be delivered when it's needed, that the customer can afford whatever price is being asked, and so on. Having a good relationship is not the *only* factor that comes into play.

Now, let's look closely at more of the variables that go into your customer's choice decision. As you read each one, think about how you could help a customer draw these conclusions if the only way you could do it was using some form of a digital asset.

To make their selection, your buyer would have to believe all or most of these statements to be true:

1. **The Trust Factor:** We know, like, and trust these people and this company.

2. **Knowledge and Insight:** These people have the knowledge and insight we need.

3. **Customer Experience:** These people honor their commitments and are easy to do business with.

4. **Stability and Reliability:** These people and their solutions have a strong track record.

5. **Product/Services Solution:** This solution is the appropriate quality and is a good fit for us.

6. **Availability and Delivery:** These people have the appropriate product selection and can deliver what we need, when we need it, and in the way that we need it delivered.

7. **Price to Value/Risk Ratio:** This solution is the best value and lowest risk option for the price.

8. **Terms and Payments:** The terms, conditions, and payment schedule are the best fit for us.

Some who read these eight statements will contend that this kind of selling might be better done in person. I totally agree! Get an appointment to sell in person whenever you can! However, that's not always easily done these days. In today's digital marketplace, buyers typically start making these kinds of judgments long before we ever have a chance to engage with them personally. We have to learn how to become the partner of choice even if we never get the chance to make our case in real-time.

Thinking back to the story I told earlier in this chapter, do you see how we created many of the videos we published to specifically address these eight points? It's absolutely possible to use text, graphics, audio, and video to address every one of these eight factors head-on and help people reach favorable conclusions about us entirely digitally. In our case, at Sales Excellence, we recognize that by providing all of this information online, we probably end up reducing the number of raw inquiries we receive from our website. Some prospects will learn enough about us to determine we are not a good fit for them or vice versa. But the leads we *do* get are exceptionally qualified, and our closure rate is extremely high.

It's important to note here that in all of your inbound selling endeavors, you are trying to help your prospects conclude these eight things about you personally as well as about your company. If you are a solopreneur, an expert, or a public figure, then you are selling yourself. Those who represent a company are selling themselves *and* their organization. Let's look at a few examples of how to do this for each of these eight areas.

1. The Trust Factor

Earning trust is accomplished in several ways. To boil it down, your prospective client has to conclude that you are a credible source, you are capable of delivering what they need, you will deal with them honestly and fairly, and that you have their best interests at heart. There are surely many other factors as well, but these are a few of the big ones.

Our prospects will begin to know, like, and trust us—or not—the moment they start consuming whatever we choose to publish. But be careful to not assume that simply racking up likes and comments on your social posts equates to earning the kind of trust people will need to actually buy something from you.

I think it's worth noting . . .

Trust is not necessarily the same thing as popularity.

Just because someone is a social influencer with 750,000 followers doesn't necessarily mean a major corporation will select him or her to partner with for a million-dollar project. It is true, however, that the opinions of others, such as fellow members of a Facebook group or fellow YouTube followers, can have a major impact on people's perceptions and beliefs about you.

"Social proof" is a key element people use to determine whom they will trust. Therefore, we have to be intentional about how we solicit and leverage the opinions of our current customers, industry experts, analysts, and yes, social followers. We then need to share those opinions for future clients to see.

Here are just a few examples of digital assets that might support earning your perspective customer's trust:

Web page dedicated to: *Our Core Beliefs as a Company and Why They Should Matter to You*

Customer testimonial: *Why* _____ *(client) Selected* _____ *(us) Over* _____ *(competitor)*

Press release: _____ *(your company) Awarded Most Trusted Company in* _____ *(geography or industry)*

Series of LinkedIn posts: *Why Choose to Partner with* _____ *(your company)*

While asynchronous selling in writing might be a new endeavor for some of us, it is *hardly* a new idea. The single most effective written selling tool I've ever created was a piece I wrote in 1996. I was working for a startup company called NTSI selling custom-built computer systems for running high-end engineering and design software. The young sales and technical pre-sales team, of which I was a part, got really good at telling the story of why companies should choose us over all of the big-name hardware manufacturers we competed with.

As I listened to our brilliant technical experts and the super-talented salespeople on our team talking to customers, I observed that our story—which resonated with our clients like crazy—boiled down to five key reasons why they should pick us. I turned those five reasons into a simple one-pager I called *Why Buy from NTSI?* We snail-mailed it to every name on our massive mailing list. We used it in all of our prospecting approaches. We built it into every presentation we gave. We even included it with every proposal. It was a tremendous success!

I think it's incredibly important to point out that I didn't come up with all the ideas in this piece myself. I happened to write it, but most of the credit for what was *in* it goes to my dear friends Tim Schmidt, Shawn Harty, Jim

Smith, Ray Zerkle, and Dave McKenna. You don't have to know it all. Gather the knowledge of the people around you and turn that into asynchronous selling tools that can earn your customers' trust when you're not even there.

2. Knowledge and Insight

Most of what your readers and viewers conclude about your knowledge and insight will be based on the assets you create and share that relate to the action drivers that were described earlier. But there could be a few other things that would draw specific attention to the value of what you know, such as the following:

Recognition: Professional designations, degrees, awards, endorsements, and certifications

Recommendations: LinkedIn recommendations from clients or respected colleagues

Customer comment: *"John brought a level of expertise and acumen that is nearly impossible to find these days. With his guidance, we were able to accomplish* _____ *in* _____ *(time frame) without having to* _____*."*

Article: *5 Things That Can Make or Break Your Next* _____ *Project.* You can then stress the importance of choosing a partner that has the right knowledge and expertise as one of the five things.

3. Customer Experience

Keep in mind that customer experience (CX) starts long before someone becomes a paying customer. The digital impressions you make before you ever even speak to clients and the way you treat them throughout the buying process are their best indicators for what it might be like to work with you. Customers need to "feel the love" from the outset and all along the journey. If they feel valued and important to you before they buy, they will naturally conclude that being your client will be a pleasant experience, too.

Always keep in mind that the voice of your current customers speaks volumes to your prospects. Make the time to collect and catalog every customer testimonial and positive comment you can get and then post them everywhere! One of the most powerful and trusted mechanisms today is recommendations and star ratings on a Google Business Profile. Every business owner should ask each happy client to rate them and leave a comment on their profile or some of other form of publicly accessible rating system. You can then take the best comments and post them on your website, LinkedIn profile, Facebook page, and so on. Try capturing some of these and turning them into digital assets designed to help you sell. Of course, don't forget about accolades and awards; they help too! Here are a few ideas for useful digital assets that emphasize customer experience:

LinkedIn post: *Thank you to all of our amazing clients who make serving them a joy, day in and day out. We are so grateful for all the wonderful reviews on Google. Check them out! (see link in first comment)*

LinkedIn post: *So excited about our partnership with _____ (tag client). Just had to share his recent testimonial with you (see below). We are honored to serve them and look forward to witnessing their success going forward!*

Press release: _____ *(your company) Recognized for "Best Customer Experience" by _____ (credible source)*

4. Stability and Reliability

To help your customer see you as the stable and reliable supplier/partner they are looking for, learn to tell your history and your story in a way that involves less bragging about your accomplishments and more about how you have served and "been there" for your current clients over a long period of time. It's true that any brand-new company could be just as safe and reliable as one that's been around for 30 years. But that is most often true because the person or the people who started it have a solid track record of success and service. This is why selling the *people* within your company and not just the company itself is so vital in earning your customer's trust. Here are a couple of assets that can help:

Press release: _____ *(your company) Announces Leading Industry Expert _____ (team member) Appointed to*

_____ *(position).* This is always a great opportunity to showcase a colleague's background and success story.

LinkedIn post about a team member: _____ *(your company) celebrates* _____ *(team member) for her 20 years of service in the* _____ *industry.* Another nice way to showcase talent and show appreciation at the same time.

White paper: *8 Things to Look for When Selecting the Best Technology Partner.* You could then emphasize stability and reliability as a critical factor.

5. Product/Services Solution

It goes without saying that the product or service that you provide is a major choice driver and a key ingredient in your customer's buying decision. What I hope to point out, however, is that there are many other factors and ways to establish value in your customer's mind and differentiate yourself from your competition. I find use cases showing exactly how your customer can use what you offer to solve specific problems they are facing to be extremely appealing. Showing your product in use via video is incredibly effective. If a picture is worth a thousand words, then a video is worth a million words!

If you have superior product features and functions, sell them! But don't forget that what makes you different in the customer's mind is how you position the capabilities of your product, not the capabilities themselves. Here are a few ways of positioning yourself as not just better, but different:

Feature video on your website: *How You Can Use* _____ *(your product or service) to Solve the 3 Most Expensive Problems for* _____ *Companies.* Here you can stress some key capabilities your competitors don't have.

Five-part email series: *5 Ways That* _____ *(your product) Is Different Than Anything Else on the Market*

YouTube video: *Side-by-Side Shootout:* _____ *(us) Versus* _____ *(them)*

I cannot resist sharing an example that I believe to be the epitome of effective competitive differentiation and earning trust using digital assets. It happens to be content on a website by the highly innovative and rapidly growing cybersecurity training company called Ninjio (www.ninjio.com). They have a tab right in the main navigation menu of their website called "Gartner Insights" where they offer side-by-side, third-party comparisons with five of their top competitors.[1]

In this case, they stack up *very* favorably to those five companies, so they would naturally put these Gartner reports front and center. You'll probably have to put some effort into this, but I want to encourage you to pick the best examples of the kind of information or statistics that set *you* apart from your competition and showcase those digitally for all to see. Ninjio posts samples of many of their training "episodes" right on their website. Watch a few and you'll see why they are getting such great reviews. What a great example of giving prospective clients a taste of what's available without forcing them to fill out a form or book an appointment!

6. Availability and Delivery

Another important factor in becoming your customer's choice is having what they need and being able to deliver it when they need it. This factor alone can win and retain business even when somebody else offers a better price or a superior product. It might not matter how superior it is if they can't deliver! Here are a couple of ways that digital content could speak to this choice driver quite nicely:

Awards: Sometimes an outside resource, like an industry magazine or newsletter, will showcase companies and even issue awards and recognition based on metrics like on-time delivery.

YouTube video: Customer testimonial talking about how your responsiveness and on-time delivery keeps them coming back for more.

Survey results: Published customer satisfaction survey showing a high percentage of on-time deliveries.

Published guarantee: Guarantee of availability and on-time deliveries. Many companies have literally made this a key element of their brand. FedEx comes to mind as does Domino's Pizza.

LinkedIn video: *How We Made Availability and Delivery the Hallmark of Our Brand.* You don't have to give away all your trade secrets, but give your customer a chance to see exactly how you are uniquely equipped to be the go-to supplier they can count on.

This is one of the things that really impressed my buyer in the story I shared at the beginning in this chapter. The ability to rapidly customize training materials was a key trigger that caused them to move forward now instead of waiting until their next fiscal year. If you have some kind of an edge over your competitors in terms of availability or your ability to deliver, this can be a huge advantage, if you sell it right.

7. Price to Value/Risk Ratio

Salespeople frequently fall for the deception that price is all that their customers care about. That's simply because customers often make comments and threats about price as a negotiation tactic to knock sellers off balance and cause them to panic. But as you can see, price is only one of eight different choice drivers listed here. It's almost never just the dollar figure that determines the decision. Instead, the choice that provides the best ratio of price to value and gives buyers the best value at the lowest *risk* most often prevails. Here are a few ways in which digital assets could be used to highlight this factor:

White paper: *Why Paying a Higher Price Can Save You Time, Money, and Embarrassment.* I love that title because "embarrassment" is a way to bring the personal ramifications of a decision into consideration.

Customer testimonial: *How _____ (client) Cut Their Costs for _____ and Lowered Their Risk at the Same Time*

LinkedIn article: *6 Ways to Get the Most Value from Your _____ Provider While Minimizing Your Exposure to _____ (risk)*

Blog post: *Why These Three Companies Chose to Partner with _____ (your company). It's All About More Value and Less Risk!*

8. Terms and Payments

This has been used as a topic for advertising for decades. Expressions like "No Money Down," "Easy Payment Terms," and "90 Days Same as Cash" have become annoyingly pervasive. But as overused as these kinds of slogans have become, the terms of our sales agreement and the timetable on which customers have to pay can be *huge* factors in swinging the choice decision this way or that. As with all the other choice drivers, we have to get creative about how to use digital assets to communicate these things to customers without it sounding like just another ad. Perhaps we could try these:

LinkedIn post: *17 Things You Can Afford to Buy Now If You Don't Have to Pay for* _____ *(your product) Until Next Year*

Article: *5 Ways to Cut Costs and Free Up Cash-Flow with Creative Financing Options*

YouTube video: *A Smarter Way to Buy: How to "Pay-by-the-Drink" for* _____ *Services*

Blog post: *3 Reasons It Doesn't Make Sense to Tie Up Working Capital for* _____ *(your product) Anymore*

Case study: *How a* _____ *Service Contract Smooths Out Cash Flow and Saves You Money*

* * *

When I am consulting and coaching people on creating content that sells, I often ask them to look back at the last 10 to 20 pieces they created and published. It might be social posts, or white papers, or email copy. Then, I ask them to identify which of these action drivers or choice drivers each piece was directed toward and what conclusions they intended for the reader or viewer to draw. I would encourage you to do the same thing. Don't just publish content for the sake of having "something to post." Develop and publish content with intent! Create content that sells!

Hopefully, you can see that what we are doing is simply taking what we might say or present to our customer in a telephone conversation or a live meeting and turning that into digital assets that can do some of the selling for us asynchronously. Many sales professionals reading this may once again think, "Our marketing department needs to be doing all of this! They are the ones that need to read this!" You might be right. Feel free to dog-ear this chapter and hand them this book with my regards.

But whether you are a sales pro, a marketer, or a small business owner that is starting to see the power of selling by using digital assets, don't wait for somebody else to do this for you. Of course, you can forge internal alliances, lobby for a cross-departmental initiative, or outsource part of this to a digital selling expert. Whatever you do, don't just hand your fate to somebody else and go back to selling and marketing the way you've always done it. Start selling the way people buy today!

Best Practices for Content Development

What I am trying to accomplish with this chapter is to persuade you that you *can* do this. You can learn to create digital assets that can be used to enable prospects to find you. You can learn to engage potential customers even if they're not willing to talk to you yet. It's going to take practice. It's going to take work.

But I'd like to stress that . . .

> **Creating content to use for either inbound demand
> generation or outbound prospecting isn't something
> you do in addition to your job. *This is your job!***

If you are thinking, "I don't have time to do this," you are not alone. I'm sure everyone who has embraced content-based selling has thought that at some point.

Here's an idea that has helped me, and it might help you, too . . .

> **If you have time to consume content, you
> have time to create content.**

I do some of my best content creation in the late evening after everyone else is asleep. I used to just browse other people's content on LinkedIn, Facebook, or YouTube to unwind at the end of the day. About a year ago, I developed a new habit of trying to write one new piece of content every night if I've got any brainpower left to do it. You may choose the early morning or whatever time works best for you. Here are a few other best practices that can help.

Become a Content Creator and Curator

Some of the content you create may be totally original thoughts and insights never before published. More often, what you'll share is *your take* on an idea or a concept that is already out there. Don't feel like everything you post has to spring from your own mind, especially to begin with.

If you are a small business owner, you know you wouldn't have even started your business if you didn't already possess some marketable skills or expertise. And even if you are a corporate sales pro who's relatively new to your company or your industry, you already know things—or will soon be learning things—that your future clients need to know.

If you don't think you have enough fresh insight and great ideas to create engaging content yourself, start collecting and curating the knowledge of others. I'll cover this in more depth in Chapter 6 on brand building, but you don't have to know it all. You never will! You can provide tremendous value to your clients when you collect and disseminate the knowledge and insight you learn from other people.

You should seek to become a source your clients can turn to for guidance and advice. If you are part of a larger organization, I am confident that your collective knowledge is enough to literally rock your customer's world. Get it out there and stop keeping all that expertise a secret.

Because of the way people buy today . . .

**If you're not intentional about curating the knowledge
and sharing the collective expertise of your team,
most people will never know it exists!**

Should only the people who are willing to travel to your facility get to meet your executive team? Should only those who've taken the leap of faith to become paying customers have a chance to learn from your world-class engineers and developers? Why not shoot a series of videos to showcase that brain trust and figure out how to enable as many people as possible to see it?

If you're only willing to share your guidance and advice with the people who are ready to take your phone call, that's going to be a small percentage of your market these days. Digitize everything you know!

You don't have to give away everything all at once. Hold some knowledge and insight back for the live conversation or the demo. Reserve some of your expertise only for your paying customers.

Remember that . . .

> **Knowledge is the new currency! If you want people you've never met to know what insight and expertise you have, you'll have to show them and tell them in some kind of digital format.**

Develop a Content Creation and Curation Plan

I'll bet some who read this will be thinking, "I've tried to spend time creating content to post on LinkedIn or YouTube, but I can never think about what I should focus on or talk about." How do you suppose I know this? For over two years I tried to create momentum on LinkedIn, but I found myself frustrated every morning trying to come up with something interesting to post.

I'd often get distracted by other tasks, and by the time I did come up with something worth posting, I'd already have missed the early morning window of time in which I wanted to post. Then I would say to myself, "Maybe I'll be able to get it done tomorrow." If this sounds familiar, please consider creating a plan and a content creation/curation schedule. It will change your life!

The key to consistency is to *not* create or curate day-to-day. That doesn't mean you can't create or curate every day. Just don't always create what you want to publish on the day you want to publish it. Instead, take 30 minutes once a month (or twice a month) and map out:

- **What do I want to publish about?** Pick some good topics or maybe a theme for the month. Think about which of the action drivers or choice drivers to focus on and how you can address them.

- **Where do I want to publish and in what format?** For example, you might decide to publish on LinkedIn each morning, do a long-form video on YouTube once a week, and write an email newsletter each month.

Then create a day-by-day plan of what topic, platform, and digital format you want to use.

After that, set aside an hour or two—or whatever you deem appropriate—each week to crank out the content. The actual time it takes to write a post or shoot a short video is usually not the problem. It's very manageable if you're not under the pressure of trying to think it up *and* produce it on the day you need to post it.

The stress of sitting there at 8:00 a.m. racking your brain for ideas while you know you've got emails sitting in your inbox and phone calls to make is just unbearable. The quality of what you create will suffer, too. Try to restrict your content creation to non-selling hours. You can use a content scheduling platform like Hootsuite (www.hootsuite.com) or Hypefury (www.hypefury.com) to release things on one or more platforms at exactly the time you want them to drop. Try it and see. You'll never go back!

Proliferate Your Content for Broader Reach

Whether you are writing your own stuff, curating the insight of others, or a combination of the two, the key to reaching a lot of people in a lot of places is content proliferation. The best way to develop a lot of content quickly is to create what I call *nested content*. You can take larger assets and break them down into a variety of smaller pieces. Keep in mind that you can start by creating brand-new digital assets or by using content that you may already have access to.

Here's the idea:

1. Pick a topic that you think has the potential to really influence your customer's thinking about one or more of the action drivers or choice drivers.

2. Create or curate a long-form piece of content, such as a 20- to 30-minute video or a 600- to 800-word article. Sales pros: get help from an expert at your company if you need to or use some content your marketing department has already created. Business owners: record yourself on video or audio and hire a contract copywriter to turn that recording into an article, if you are unable to write it yourself. Post the video on YouTube. Post the article on your website blog or as an article on LinkedIn.

3. Slice that one video asset into a half-dozen 3- to 4-minute videos to post on LinkedIn or Facebook. Break the article down into several smaller pieces of 80 to 120 words for short posts on your choice of platform. If an article is made up of three major points, you can release one each day for the next three days.

4. Take the best one-liners from both and post them on Twitter.

You don't have to create everything as separate pieces. Learn how to create something more substantial for people who are ready and willing to consume long-form content and break it down into multiple pieces of short-form content for those who just want a light snack. My best one-liners are sentences that I take from the longer pieces I create. A great example of that are the "pull quotes" (bolded sentences that are set apart) used throughout this book itself.

When I began writing this book, I decided to launch a one-hour weekly live-video meeting that I called the *Sales Excellence Show* where I committed myself to complete and present new material on digital selling every week. I invited a few hundred people to attend when they could at no charge. It was the perfect way to test-drive the new material and hold myself accountable to produce it.

We recorded and then posted all the shows on a private website, started a collection of the various sales tools I presented, and turned all of that into a membership community we called the *Sales Excellence Insider's Club*. We then sliced up the one-hour recordings into dozens of short videos that we could post on LinkedIn and other platforms to promote the show. We also lifted literally hundreds of little 160-character nuggets that we called *Text Tips* and sent them via automated text message to all of our members several times a week. Almost everything in this book originated from the first 25 episodes of that show.

* * *

All corporate sales professionals who want to embrace selling with digital assets can start by taking inventory of everything they already have available to them in terms of platforms and content. In many cases, your marketing department will have more material than you could ever possibly use, *but . . .* it may not be insight-oriented content designed to actually *sell*.

A lot of the marketing content that is produced revolves around your products and services instead of your customers' desired outcomes and results. It might be focused on positioning your company as the best *choice* for your customer but have nothing at all to do with the conclusions that customers have to draw to make their *action* decision. Use it anyway until you and/or your marketing team can make more "content with intent" to add to it! This is where marketing and sales have to work together to win together!

Choose to see this as an awesome opportunity to create some fresh new material. Of course, those who want outside help can look to an agency to take on the bulk of this effort. Some small business owners may do part of this themselves and seek out a freelancer using a professional services marketplace like Upwork (www.upwork.com) or Fiverr (www.fiverr.com) to get help polishing things up or breaking things down into chunks.

But let me make this point . . .

Whether you create your digital assets yourself or hand that job to someone else, *you* have to make sure the finished product is designed to actually sell by shaping perception and influencing your customer's thinking and behavior.

Hand off or outsource the creative work as you deem necessary, but don't completely turn over the responsibility of digital selling to another department or an outside resource. I seriously doubt you'll be happy with the result. Get involved in the creation of your content and build in the kinds of questions, stories, case studies, and insights that you would share if you were literally talking to your customer in real time.

In fact, one of the best ways to start capturing what you want to say in your digital sales content is to start recording the conversations you have with your customers and prospects. Listen back to the three reasons you told them why they should choose you over your competitor and turn it into an article. Transcribe your explanation of why your customer might not want to wait two more months to get started and write a LinkedIn post about it. Or maybe record your conversation on video and post it on YouTube. Turn your sales savvy and persuasion expertise into digital selling tools!

The big idea here is . . .

> **Selling via digital content should be the
> asynchronous equivalent of whatever you would
> normally say to your customer on a telephone
> conversation or in a face-to-face meeting.**

Putting These Ideas into Practice

**To make practical use of what we've talked about in this chapter,
make the time to:**

1. *Look Back at the Last 10 to 20 Pieces You Created and Published*

   Think about the intent of each piece. What did you want your customer to think differently or do differently after they read or watched it? If that's not entirely clear, how could you change the format or substance to make it more intentional? If you haven't done much in the way of publishing content yet, then go out and look at some examples from other individuals or companies in your space. This is a great way to get some ideas of what you can do—or even what *not* to do.

2. *Select Two or More Action Drivers or Choice Drivers to Focus on Next*

   As you look through the lists of eight action drivers and eight choice drivers, choose two or more of each to give some attention to. They might be areas that you've never really tried to address with your

(continued)

content before or areas where you have a very compelling story to tell that you just haven't told yet.

3. *Choose a Format and Create Some Things That Are Designed to Influence and Persuade*

Pick a format and a channel, such as an article to post on LinkedIn or a video to post on YouTube, and make something. Don't even try to make it perfect. Just start something and finish it. Of course, the hardest part is getting started. But finishing can also be a challenge! The key to developing your skill and confidence is simply *doing it.*

4. *Publish It Right Now!*

This step is the scariest step. Most everyone struggles with, "What will people think of me?" Honestly, most people don't have time to think about judging you. They are too busy worrying about how other people are judging them. Take the step you know you need to take in spite of the fear.

5. *If You Can't Bring Yourself to Publish It, Commit to Coming Back and Making It Better Soon*

If you simply are not willing or able to post it, then set it aside and come back with a fresh mind a couple of days later. Seek some input and feedback from someone on your team or an outside resource you trust. Make a couple of improvements and put it out there for the world to see. You'll get better with every piece you create. Everybody has to start somewhere!

CHAPTER 4

Designing Your Digital Selling Engine

Many of us grew up in the world of outside, outbound selling. Not all that long ago that was basically our only choice! I love to make people laugh in my workshops by sharing stories about my early days swinging by the bank to pick up rolls of quarters so I could stop at a pay phone to make follow-up calls on the way to my next appointment. It seems like the Dark Ages, but we closed millions of dollars in revenue every year before websites and email ever existed.

Although that's where I started out, I certainly did *not* stay there. What is shocking to me is how many in this profession—even some half my age—are stuck in what I affectionately refer to as "old-school selling." It went something like this:

First, we'd do everything imaginable to collect names and contact information. We bought mailing lists or set up booths at trade shows and exchanged tchotchkes for business cards. Entire marketing departments existed primarily to collect people's contact information to be handed over to the sales team as "leads." Once a salesperson had someone's contact info, they would employ some combination of letters, faxes, emails, telephone calls, or drop-bys to try to initiate a conversation. Every touch via every medium was an attempt to schedule a meeting.

Once we got *in front* of somebody, or at least got them on the phone, we would start selling. The intent of the conversation, of course, was to close a sale or at least close on *something*. I've spent most of my sales career selling big-ticket solutions, so many times my *win* in any meeting was simply closing on another opportunity to meet with my customer. Old-school selling consisted primarily of what I call the Three C's: contact, conversation, and close.

Today, a very affordable online subscription to a contact search and lead generation service like Seamless.AI (www.seamless.ai) or a broader go-to-market intelligence platform like ZoomInfo (www.zoominfo.com) can give you extensive contact details for nearly every person you'd ever want to meet. You can search for companies and contacts by specific locations, industries, titles, and a variety of other characteristics. Developing a list of contacts is no longer the bottleneck in sales prospecting.

Most of us can observe, however, that the return on investment for cold-call prospecting to an acquired contact list is not what it once was. I recently saw a study of hundreds of sales reps making thousands of cold calls that showed the following success ratios:[1]

- 330 attempted telephone calls
- 59 calls answered
- 1 appointment booked

Maybe those numbers are typical for some sales environments, but that seemed absolutely *abysmal* to me. Of course, you can use some form of sales automation to accelerate the process. Using an auto dialer system, you could probably accomplish that pretty quickly. But I can't help but think about what could be done to engage the 271 contacts who didn't answer the phone. I also wonder:

1. What could have been said or asked differently to influence and engage more of the 58 people who did answer but did not agree to an appointment?
2. What other action, short of booking an appointment, might those 58 have been willing to take if they had been given the option?

Through the next two chapters, we'll be talking about creating a business development strategy comprised of both inbound and outbound sales motions that will enable you to build e-relationships that pave the way for more productive and fruitful conversations whenever your prospects are willing to have them. We'll also explore a wide variety of ways to engage at least some of the 329 legitimate "suspects" in the previous example that did not agree to an appointment just yet.

As a reminder, this is a handbook, not a novel. If you are super excited about building a magnetic personal brand, feel free to jump right to Chapter 6. If you need help *right now* on the strategies and tactics of outbound digital prospecting, go ahead and proceed to Chapter 7. When you want to learn more about how to leverage inbound demand-generation strategies to build a following of people who want to become your next prospect, come on back. These next two chapters will still be here for you.

Taking Ownership of Your Business

When I'm working with business owners, marketing teams, or individual salespeople on developing their overall digital selling strategy, I sometimes hear, "I can't do all the things you are talking about!" The entrepreneur might conclude that they are just not cut out to be a videographer or a copywriter. As a small business owner myself, I encourage you not to limit yourself. Don't tell yourself it's impossible before you ever start. You don't have to do it all. You can hire or outsource the skills you don't have time to develop, and you can probably barter some of your own products and services in exchange for many of them.

The individual salesperson or sales leader working for a larger company is often quick to point out, "We have a marketing department that does all of that." Well, let's ask ourselves a question: Who's responsible for sales results? Whose income and perhaps even job security are tied to achieving specific revenue targets? That's who is ultimately responsible!

Whether you are running a business or selling for one, remember this: a marketing department, a business development team, or an outsourced lead generation function are simply resources to you. The person who owns the revenue number needs to intimately understand all the digital selling touchpoints—all the pieces your prospects see throughout the customer relationship journey. It doesn't mean you have to do it all. You may not be able to call all the shots. But knowing how all the pieces work together and learning to leverage them to achieve your goals is paramount.

Because I had an entrepreneurial background, this came natural to me. Early on in my corporate sales career I adopted a *Business-Within-a-Business*

(BWB) mentality. I paid for my own computer and whatever software applications I needed. I bought my own prospect lists and covered the cost of sending prospecting letters via FedEx to target executives (best approach ever, by the way). I even hired a part-time assistant to take as many administrative tasks off my plate as possible—on my own nickel.

If you have a geographic territory, a vertical market, or a set of named accounts you are responsible for, then everything that your company does with those customer organizations is *your business*. Take responsibility for building your own business, your reputation and credibility, as well as your own brand as an expert in your field. See yourself as the executive in charge of helping your customers succeed, even if you need a team of nine other people internally to do it.

The problem is . . .

> **If you see yourself and manage your territory as "just one of the reps" at your company, then your customer will only ever see you as "just another rep" and therefore someone they'll probably try to avoid.**

Sales pros: if you've got a rock star marketing team that is doing everything we're talking about in this book, that's awesome! Partner with them and crush your goals together. But if you don't, or you've only got a few pieces in place to work with, then build your overall strategy out of what you have and add in the missing pieces yourself.

For marketing pros and sales enablement leaders who see the need to create digital selling assets like we've been talking about, find someone in sales leadership who will buy into this approach and work with them to fully equip the sales team for asynchronous selling.

Your Digital Selling Engine

An effective digital selling strategy is composed of a combination of inbound and outbound selling mechanisms that fit your business model and sales environment. I call this your *digital selling engine*. The engine for an online retailer will look entirely different from that of a professional services firm and different yet from the sales engine of a high-tech manufacturer.

The engine is designed to empower customers at every stage of their buying cycle and lead them through a customer relationship journey. This includes the period of time before they even get to Point A, where they recognize or acknowledge any kind of pain, problem, or need. A great digital engine also keeps customers engaged after they buy something at Point B, turning them into repeat clients, advocates, and even champions that actively recommend us to others.

To make this idea easy to understand and implement, I break the digital selling engine down into four layers as follows:

1. **Connection Layer:** This is where we make connections with people we don't yet know or who don't yet know us. We may use inbound strategies to drive traffic to a destination like a website, a blog, or a posted video. We might make social connections and attract people to our social media profiles. We may also utilize various outbound strategies to reach out to people by telephone, email, text, or direct messages through social channels.

2. **Conversion Layer:** This is the layer where connections, followers, or visitors can be converted to some deeper relationship. It could be as simple as exchanging their email address for a free digital asset that provides valuable insight. For more complex selling environments, the conversion might result in a formal request for information or a scheduled time to speak by live video or telephone.

3. **Selling Layer:** This is where selections are made, commitments are made, contracts are signed, etc. Depending on the nature of your business, this might be done completely online, through personal interaction between a buyer and a seller, or a combination of the two. Completing more complex sales transactions would also likely require demonstrations, presentations, proposals, and negotiations.

4. **Retention and Repeat Layer:** This is where the *next* sale is made. The importance of this layer cannot be overstated. I'm convinced this represents the single greatest opportunity for growth for just about any business. We've all probably heard the statistics about how much less expensive it is to make a second sale to an existing

client than it is to attract a new one. It also often takes far less time
and energy when we can basically skip the connection stage and
sometimes even the conversion stage en route to the next transaction.

Here is an important point: all of this *can* be done via telephone. For
decades it was! But today's buyer wants and even expects to be able to get
to know us, work through a discovery process, and maybe even compare us
to other providers without talking to us by phone, if they choose. A solid
digital selling engine allows them to do that. Plus, it's more scalable. There
are only so many phone calls you can make and people you can talk to in a
day. But by leveraging the right digital assets, your reach and capacity can
increase exponentially.

This chapter was written to be a bit of an overview of some of the most
common platforms and tools you can employ as part of your digital selling
strategy. In the next chapter, we will focus on how we use these various
components to engage people and foster e-relationships as we lead them
through the customer relationship journey. Now, let's talk about the different tools we might need in order to digitize as much of this as possible.

Assembling Your Digital Selling Engine

At the risk of being overwhelming, I want to show you a picture of what
a comprehensive digital selling engine could look like in Figure 4.1. Hang
in there with me! We'll sort all this out together. Note the four layers: connection, conversion, selling, and retention. Note there are both inbound and
outbound motions shown in the connection layer (top layer). Also notice a
variety of other components that function in the other three layers, which
we'll unpack as we go.

Of course, no two engines look the same, nor do they need to. What
works best for you and your company will be unique based on what you
sell, who you sell to, how they buy, and—not the least of which—the strategies that you feel confident will work for you. You certainly don't need to
employ all of these pieces, but you need *at least one* mechanism in each
of the four layers that you consistently use to create new sales opportunities, close deals, and drive repeat business. You can expand your capacity
from there.

Figure 4.1   Components of Your Digital Selling Engine

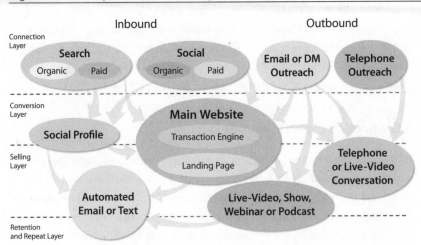

Please keep in mind the fact that smaller organizations may not use all of these mechanisms. If you are an individual salesperson for a company with a marketing department, some of these pieces may not be under your direct control. However, it's important that every seller understands the engine they have at their disposal and how to use it to find, create, and close new business.

We'll talk about each of the different pieces shown here as we go forward. By the end of this chapter, you'll have a much clearer idea of where you are today. You also might feel a conviction to improve what you are doing in one or more of these areas or to add certain tools to your arsenal.

As we discussed in the earlier chapters, when you earnestly step into the world of digital selling, you essentially decide to become a media company. If you fully embrace what is being said here, you'll take almost everything that you historically would ask or say to your customer—and nearly everything you would show them along the way—and capture that in one or more digital formats. These assets could take the form of written messages, graphic images, audio, or video. Then you'll be able to serve up those digital assets at the right time in a variety of delivery vehicles, some inbound and some outbound, as the situation calls for.

You can learn to tell your company history in writing and photos. You can learn to showcase client success stories and use cases via video. You can create an infographic that helps differentiate you from your competitors. You can even continually challenge your customers' thinking and share new ideas with them via an automated email list. As you create your digital asset library, you can use all these tools to keep selling to your customers before, during, and after any personal interaction. By doing so, you allow your customers to take steps in their buying process 24/7/365.

The Connection Layer (Inbound)

If you want to leverage inbound lead generation strategies, there are two major channels that generate the majority of new connections: search and social. Of course, there are other mechanisms that can be used to attract new connections, such as podcasting, for example. But even the fastest-growing podcasts attract the majority of their new subscribers via search and social. First, let's talk about search, then social in two different forms—organic and paid.

Organic Search

Search is all about leveraging *keywords*. Every sales pro or business owner needs to know the keyword phrases that their prospective clients are typing into search engines as they relate to the kinds of solutions they provide. If you have responsibility or influence over what's on your website, make it your business to continuously optimize your site to be found by people searching for what you can deliver.

Search engine optimization (SEO) is a topic far too broad to address in this book, but your website—or wherever you intend to drive search traffic to—needs to be designed with the specific intent of being attractive to search engines. Your website also has to be designed to convert that traffic, which we'll talk more about later on.

If you happen to have little or no influence over what's on your website, let's remember that all the major search engines also index articles hosted anywhere online as well as blog posts, LinkedIn articles and posts, and YouTube videos. Creating and posting content that is rich with keywords and valuable insight is within reach of any salesperson or business owner who's willing to produce and publish it.

Perhaps you sell telecommunication equipment or services. Are your prospects going to Google to search for "5G"? That's probably far too vague. They may never find you among the millions of other destinations on the web talking about 5G.

If you want to think more like your customer, ask yourself this: What is 5G, and what does it promise? Your potential customers who are in the early stages of discovery are more likely typing in "5G explained" or "benefits of 5G." They might be further along and searching "fastest wireless in Chicago" or "most reliable wireless network in Denver." They could also get very specific with something like "reduce wireless lag time and latency" or "compare costs of landline vs. fixed wireless access."

Take the responsibility to know the keywords your prospective clients are typing in. If you have marketing support, seek to understand their organic search strategy. There are many services to help with defining keywords. Semrush (www.semrush.com) is a great one. WordStream (www.wordstream.com) also offers some great free tools for keyword research. For other options, just Google "best keywords to use for _____ (fill in the blank) industry." Irony intended. The idea is to identify a handful of keyword strings for which you'd like to be known and build content and insight that is laden with those keywords.

We should also be weaving keywords into our emails and direct messages (DMs). Write email subject lines and bullet points about the very phrases your prospective clients are already curious about. Remember to use words related to customer outcomes (Point C) and not just your products and services (B). Every web page, online article, blog entry, or social post should be titled and written containing the keywords your customers are typing into the search bar.

Have you noticed that when you type pretty much anything into Google these days you see a list of Frequently Asked Questions (FAQs) that relate to whatever you type? One of today's most effective SEO strategies is to create content that answers the questions most often asked on any given topic. A blog post on something like "What are the advantages of 5G wireless?" or "What are the pros and cons of fixed wireless access?" could be written to answer specific questions potential customer are asking.

One of the most underutilized and therefore untapped opportunities is organic search for video. YouTube is actually the world's second-largest search engine next to Google. Most of what comes up in a YouTube search is organic. Some highly competitive keywords will have paid links from Google at the top and, of course, nearly every video posted today has "pre-roll" video ads out front. But the potential for organic reach on You-Tube is tremendous.

YouTube also indexes based on the words you say *within* your video using speech recognition technology. So, I recommend writing the script for your video ahead of time to focus on and include specific keywords you are trying to target. Create a transcript of your video using Scribie (www.scribie.com) or some other online transcription service and make sure to upload that (or a portion of it) in the notes section with your video. Also use hashtags including your target keywords and other terms for which you wish to be found. Just go onto YouTube and type in "How to drive traffic on YouTube." There is more advice there than you could fit in 50 books.

Paid Search

What made Google the behemoth it is today is AdWords, which is now known as Google Ads. In the early days, the return on investment of AdWords could not be matched. It was the shortcut to be found at the top of the page for every Google search. You could bid a couple of bucks on a certain keyword phrase in the morning and have leads streaming in throughout the day. I built my business for the first 10 years with a heavy emphasis on AdWords and saw a 10x to 20x return on marketing investment every year.

Today, paid search—or pay-per-click (PPC) as it is often called—is much more competitive and requires a more serious strategic commitment. But when you want traffic or leads that are in that Top 3 percent and are literally searching for what you offer, paid search is still incredibly effective. As I said in Chapter 1, "People who are looking to buy now use search." Many experts argue that SEO is a more cost-effective long-term strategy. But when done right PPC search produces leads now!

The key to being found in a cost-effective way via paid search is the use of "long-tail keywords." In my world, for example, the term "sales training" gets a *ton* of traffic. However, that term is so broad that many of the people who click on the listing (which can cost $10 or more per click) aren't really viable prospects that convert to opportunities anyway.

More specific keywords such as "sales prospecting training for SDRs" or "negotiation training for sales managers" often allow you to be seen more cost-effectively and result in more high-quality visitors. The same is true for organic traffic. I've actually had good success by focusing on keywords that describe desired outcomes (Point C instead of B). A phrase like "increase lead conversion" or "improve forecast accuracy" or even "close more sales" can bring visitors who already know what they want to accomplish.

Organic Social

By far the least expensive way to start leveraging inbound sales strategies is organic social media. You can immediately start making connections first with people you already know and then with others you'll find and meet along the way. The two most popular platforms for most businesses are Facebook and LinkedIn. Pick the one where your customers are most likely to hang out, keeping in mind that LinkedIn is the service people often use to learn and talk about business while Facebook tends to be more recreational.

Posting is easy and free! You can begin expressing your opinions, starting conversations, and sharing content immediately. Of course, you can put up advertising-type posts and undoubtedly find some prospects. But as discussed in the previous chapter, people today respond far better to insight and ideas that they can actually use. The most popular content creators are those who regularly post free material to help educate, inform, and even entertain their present and future clients. They don't just pitch their products or services every day.

Organic social can be a fabulous way to consistently make new connections, grow your professional network, and even create a following. Just keep in mind that setting up your profile properly, connecting with the right people, attracting the right followers, and consistently nourishing your following with high-quality insight and ideas takes a significant amount of time and attention. There is no magic, simple, or easy way to grow a sizable following. It takes either time or money. Much more on how to do this in Chapter 5.

Paid Social

Paying for social exposure can be another very cost-effective means of advertising today. The true beauty of social media advertising is the ability to target who sees your content. You can target people on Facebook by a variety of demographic variables and even by their personal interests. You can also upload a list of email addresses and ask the system to produce a target list of "lookalike" profiles of other people who share characteristics of those on your list.

If you are using LinkedIn, you can leverage their powerful Navigator tool (available to paid subscribers), where you can literally sort out the specific individuals you want to put your ads in front of. It's amazing to have the ability to focus all your resources on targeting exactly those people you want to build relationships with. Whether you are using paid ads or just want to use LinkedIn to quickly find prospects that fit your ideal customer profile, sign up for LinkedIn Navigator. If your company won't cover the cost, pay for it yourself!

I certainly understand the natural resistance to pay for social media exposure. If you are a salesperson for a company, you might never even consider it at this point. But I may persuade you otherwise when we get to Chapter 6 on personal branding. For business owners and professional marketeers who are not already leveraging paid social, I encourage you to explore it. Get the guidance and help of an experienced professional if you need it. But you don't need an advertising firm and a huge budget to get in the game.

Facebook ads can be a very inexpensive way to simply attract page followers, for example, but your overall cost per client acquisition is something you'll have to test in order to determine if you are satisfied with the results. One common complaint, for example, is "LinkedIn advertising is really expensive." If you look at raw costs per click, it may be quite a bit higher than Facebook or other options. But you have to look beyond cost-per-click and focus on how many of those clicks become paying customers. CPA (cost per acquisition) of a new customer is what you want to look at.

Most growth-minded companies eventually embrace the fact that it costs either money or someone's personal time to consistently get your content in front of your ideal prospects on social. Since time is so incredibly limited, many companies would do well to adopt a strategy that can produce leads *on-demand* for money. You will eventually run out of time, but if you are getting a great ROI, you can grow your investment in paid social as you grow revenue. For those willing to make the financial investment, paid social can give you immediate, highly targeted reach and exposure.

The Connection Layer (Outbound)

Inbound lead generation is obviously not the only way to cultivate relationships and make new connections. Outbound prospecting is still alive and well for any who are willing to do the work! Outbound engagement can be synchronous, in the case of a live telephone conversation, or asynchronous, in the form of written, audio, or video assets sent to prospects via some delivery mechanism.

Sadly, the way so many organizations are using outbound these days is becoming increasingly ineffective and downright annoying to prospects. Best practices such as research and preparation, genuine empathy, conversational discovery, and a desire to actually help people are being abandoned for the sake of expedience and playing the numbers game "at scale." We have to rethink our strategy and get creative in our approaches if we want to remain relevant among the ever expanding "noise" in the marketplace. We'll cover much more on prospecting strategy in Chapter 7.

Outbound Telephone Connections

As crazy as this sounds, outbound telephone calls can be a "secret weapon" in our current digital-first marketplace. Fewer salespeople seem to be willing to make telephone calls these days. That's a good thing for those of us who are willing! The reluctance could be just a good old-fashioned lack of confidence in themselves and what they sell. Or maybe they just don't have faith that the reward is worth the risk of being ignored or rejected.

It's true, many customers would probably rather not receive a sales call, but that doesn't mean we should abandon the practice altogether. We simply need to do it really well, test and perfect an approach that works, and be willing to take some noes on our way to find the yeses! And remember that the effectiveness of telephone calls can be amplified dramatically with some form of a connection or correspondence with the prospect *before* you make the call.

Making a surprise telephone call when your prospective client least expects it can still work, especially in certain sales environments. I will never stop making calls to strangers when it seems like the best approach. But that's no longer the only method I use to approach people I don't already know.

For my own prospecting work, and that of so many salespeople I train and coach, setting up a time for a scheduled conversation consistently produces a more positive outcome than simply hitting people out of the blue. The question is: how do you get those appointments? That's where using inbound strategies or outbound approaches via email and direct messaging come into play.

Outbound Email and Direct Messages

Despite its frequent overuse or misuse, email can still be a terrific medium for getting people's attention, selling asynchronously, and booking appointments. The belief that most prospects totally ignore or instantly delete emails from people they don't already know is a gross overgeneralization.

In fact, a well-crafted email that talks about your customer and their business (not about you and your business) is likely to stand in contrast to the dozens or hundreds of emails they receive every day from their internal colleagues and obvious spammers. Here again, it's the substance of what is *in* the email that determines its effectiveness. But just because they look at your email does not necessarily mean they are going to respond to it or do anything with it.

The long-standing marketing rule of thumb was that it took an average of seven advertising impressions before a prospective client really took notice. Recent statistics suggest that these days it's more like 10 to 12. In the same way, outbound prospecting usually takes multiple attempts before you get a response.

That being said, an automated sequence of emails that are little more than a string of advertisements or an incessant series of requests for a telephone appointment are often ignored, deleted, or marked as spam. Your message has to add value! It needs to deliver insight, information, and aha moments that cause the reader to think differently than they thought before they read it. You have to *sell* people on why they should make the time to talk to you.

Later on, I'll show you how to weave together a multipronged approach that includes a variety of media such as FedEx letters, direct messages via LinkedIn, voicemail, handwritten notes, text messaging, and many others. This will increase your likelihood of getting noticed exponentially.

* * *

Throughout all of our efforts to make new connections either inbound or outbound, we have to be careful not to fall into the trap of playing the "numbers game" or chasing vanity metrics. The number of social followers we have or the number of likes and comments you receive for social posts are useless if they never convert into viable prospects and sales. Likewise, the number of telephone dials you make in a day or even the number of people who answer their phone doesn't always directly translate to revenue.

The whole reason you make connections is to eventually convert them into something beyond just a connection. Conversion is the key! Let's talk about that.

The Conversion Layer

There are several different mechanisms for converting connections, as shown in the second layer of Figure 4.1. One of them, of course, is a live telephone conversation. This might result from a prospect proactively contacting you in response to something they found through search or social. It might also be a reply to an email or voicemail. But inbound telephone calls from prospects are becoming much harder to come by. You can obviously also drive impromptu conversations by making outbound telephone calls.

Many of the most effective telephone conversations occur—and much deeper exploration happens—after a prospective client visits one or more online destinations such as a website, a social profile, or an online sales funnel designed to convert the connection into a conversation.

In recent years, sales funnels or "lead funnels" have become incredibly popular. Basically, a funnel is a streamlined website (landing page) designed for the express purpose of converting visitors into leads. Many companies use lead funnels in lieu of or in conjunction with a traditional website. Definitely keep in mind that your social profile can also act as a very effective conversion device if it's written for this purpose. If you don't have any control over what's on your company website, your LinkedIn profile can be made into a powerful lead funnel. More on that later.

Live Video or Telephone Conversation

Given the option, I'd prefer live video conversations to any other mechanism if I can't meet with my prospect face-to-face. I really enjoy meeting and talking with new people. But it's not just personal preference. It's also because many of the projects we deliver for our corporate clients are highly tailored professional services. Nearly every major engagement is custom configured based on the client's specific needs, goals, and objectives. So, a live conversation to talk about all of that is ideal.

However, in recent years we have proven that enabling e-conversations with our prospective clients before an initial live conversation has been a game changer. I am stunned by how much of the sales conversation we now have with our prospective clients happens asynchronously. Our customers love it! They want to be able to watch videos, look at options, and even test-drive some of our online programs from their smartphone whenever they chose to visit our website.

If what you sell simply demands a telephone conversation, I get it. But we've found that by making at least part of what we would say or ask in that live discussion available online, our prospects are able to get a feel for how we can help them even before we talk. When we do this, two amazing things happen.

First, this gives the client a chance to check us out a bit before they commit to the conversation. This results in even more people choosing to have that live discussion than if we ask them to meet with us cold. Second, the quality of those conversations is much richer. We have some common ground based on what they've seen and read. And after they've watched a bit of video prior to a live conversation, they feel like they are talking to someone they already know.

While a real-time discussion may well be the ultimate opportunity to "sell," we've found that the asynchronous selling that can be done via digital assets before the call happens can improve the likelihood of success *on* the call. More of those calls convert into sales opportunities and closed projects.

Once again, there are only so many 15- or 30-minute slots on your calendar each week. Wouldn't you rather fill them up with people who have already drawn some favorable conclusions about you and have chosen to meet with you to take the next step in the exploration?

Your Company Website

The true heart of your digital selling engine is your company website—or at least it should be! I still find small business owners who operate with only a Facebook profile and a business card. But, in most cases, if you want to grow beyond what I refer to as a "friends and family" business, you're going to need a website where people can get to know you and better understand what you can do to help them.

The good news is that it doesn't have to be elaborate or expensive. You can build your first website yourself with an inexpensive tool like Squarespace (www.squarespace.com) or Wix (www.wix.com). Either of those will get you up and running. You might choose to go upmarket a bit and invest in a site built on a platform like WordPress (www.wordpress.com) or something even more powerful and flexible than that. For most small businesses, a WordPress site will do most of what you'll ever need a website to do. I always suggest starting simple and upgrading to a custom site when you need to.

What's most important about your website is not the platform it's built on but the content within it and its ability to convert traffic. Your website is where people will read the sales copy that you write. It's where you will embed videos for people to watch even if those videos happen to be hosted on YouTube. It's where visitors can download a free report, a free guide, or a checklist that provides valuable insight.

Your website should be your primary conversion tool. A great website converts visitors from one stage of the customer journey to the next by enabling them to do as many of the following as possible:

- Follow you on any social platform where you have a presence
- Subscribe to your YouTube channel
- Subscribe to your email list
- Subscribe to your blog
- Join a discussion group or online forum
- Download a digital asset in exchange for their contact information
- Register for an upcoming webinar or masterclass
- Book an appointment with you
- Contact you by email, telephone, or live chat
- Request additional information
- Enroll in an online course you offer
- Sign up for a free trial
- Buy now!
- Leave a customer review

Each of these actions that your website enables moves your customers forward and deepens their relationship with you, which we will explore further in the next chapter. If your website doesn't enable your prospective clients to do most or all of what's listed here, you might need to add some capabilities to support today's more digital buying behavior.

For now, let's embrace this critical point . . .

Your website needs to be more than just an online brochure. It should be designed with the intent of propelling visitors through their digital buying process.

Creative companies are using custom landing pages not just for certain product lines or specific vertical industries. Some of my clients are adding pages for individual salespeople designed to foster e-relationships and convert visitors into meaningful connections and conversations in all the ways described throughout this book.

You might be saying, "My company's website is terrible! I have no hope!" Please step back from the ledge. Thousands of salespeople will hit their quotas this year with an awful website. I'm just giving you an idea of what great looks like.

Social Profiles

Your social profile can be an outstanding mechanism for converting strangers into followers and visitors into subscribers. A great social profile should be designed just like a landing page of a website with conversion in mind. You can post nearly any kind of digital asset there and start publishing your insights immediately.

Your LinkedIn profile, for example, could be one of the most valuable pieces of digital real estate you could ever have. This is especially true if you are a corporate sales pro and you don't have your own blog or website where people can find you or you can publish content. You can do all of that right on LinkedIn. You can even publish your own newsletter to which your followers can subscribe.

Go out to Google and search your own name; there's a good chance your LinkedIn profile will come up as the very first listing, or at least within the first few. Try it right now and see if I'm right. When you type my name into Google, my LinkedIn profile is the first link displayed at the very top. It appears above Amazon.com, where my books have been listed since 2004, and even above my own company's website!

Invest the time to optimize your LinkedIn profile to be a captivating destination for people who happen to search your name as well as anyone who reads one of your articles or posts. Our research, surveying thousands of active LinkedIn users, shows that 88 percent of them "routinely" visit a person's profile before they decide whether to accept a request to connect or agree to a live conversation. Incredible!

Start by fully completing your profile. Both LinkedIn and Facebook offer guidance on the various sections available. Leverage every field you can to share what your customers can accomplish by working with you. This is especially important when it comes to the imagery you use throughout the profile and the posts, videos, or articles you choose to feature.

Notice I didn't say use every field to talk about yourself. Just like everything we've discussed so far, your social profile shouldn't be about what you do. It should be about what your customer can do with your help. You can feature written or video testimonials and recommendations from your clients and even offer free digital assets that are designed to foster awareness and build e-relationships.

For more ideas on creating a profile that is fine-tuned for conversion, download my free guide *How to Optimize Your LinkedIn Profile to Attract Followers and Convert Leads Like Crazy* at: www.salesexcellence.com /handbook.

The Selling Layer

Put simply, the selling layer is where you connect the dots between what your client needs and wants and what you have to offer. It's where you:

- Earn trust and rapport
- Position yourself and your value promise
- Present the buyer with options
- Overcome any obstacles standing in their way
- Mitigate risk in the buyer's mind
- Ask for a commitment

Let's just take a quick look at the two main ways this is done: either via personal interaction with customers or entirely digitally.

Meetings, Telephone Calls, and Live Video Calls

For many environments, especially in the world of professional services or complex technology solutions, selling takes one or more live conversations at some point. This is especially true where you need to:

- Conduct some form of discovery or needs analysis
- Build relationships and rapport with the various stakeholders involved in the buying decision
- Bring other key people from your company into the conversation
- Collaborate on an implementation plan or delivery schedule
- Present a custom presentation or proposal
- Negotiate contract terms and conditions
- Close on a commitment to move forward

In this type of sales environment, leveraging digital assets to help customers make decisions and draw new conclusions—even between meetings—can turn more of those meetings into closed deals. We'll talk extensively about the digital assets we'll need for selling complex solutions in Chapter 8.

Online or Fully Digital Selling

In a strictly online selling environment, most or all of your selling is done on one or more "sales pages." This is where carefully worded "sales copy" would, in essence, lead your customer through the same series of questions you'd ask if you were sitting in front of them or speaking by phone. You'd share the same kinds of examples and use cases. You'd present your recommendations and even handle objections (perhaps presented as frequently asked questions) all with the written word, graphics, and video.

What if you could so effectively lead your customers through their buying process online that they'd either buy right there or call you up ready to buy? I encourage you to ask yourself this question: How much of what I would normally ask or say in a live conversation could I turn into some digital asset that my client could access asynchronously?

Many old-school sellers might cringe at this suggestion. As I said earlier, you lose some of your perceived "control" when you allow people to consume information and gain insight asynchronously. But if you don't put the content out there, someone else will. You don't have to publish every-thing. You can strategically hold back key bits of information that can only be obtained by speaking with you live.

Of course, the ideal situation for many of us would be to figure out how to sell more of what we offer in an online, self-service model where people can buy without having to talk to anyone. This is why we've invested so much energy into building our Sales Excellence Academy (www.academy.salesexcellence.com), where people can buy our online courses and even some of our blended course options right on our website. For markets where this is a possibility, why not explore how you could empower your clients to buy at least some of the things you offer entirely digitally?

The Retention and Repeat Layer

There is a strong psychological tendency in business to always feel like we need more *new* customers. In some cases we do. But in just as many cases, salespeople and business owners tend to fail miserably at taking care of the customers they *already have*. There are two reasons why this is a huge mistake.

The first reason is obvious. If a person or a company has already spent money with you—assuming you've held up your end of the bargain and delivered as promised—the next sale is simply a matter of helping them recognize the needs they may have at their *new* current state (Point A), envisioning their *new* desired future state (Point C), and presenting the next logical solution (your new B).

Don't forget that your customer will always have the next need that begs to be filled. If you don't stay engaged to help them achieve their next goal or objective, your competitors gladly will.

My best advice for repeat business has always been . . .

> **Treat your existing clients like brand-new clients. No matter how you've helped them in the past, reassess where they're at *now*, where they want to go *next*, and offer a way to get there.**

The second reason you need to take better care of your existing clients is that some of them may become advocates and even champions who can

provide great reviews and testimonials. Some will even become an extension of your sales team and actively refer business to you!

Our existing customer base is a highly coveted asset, so . . .

> **We should be working at least as hard to keep our existing
> customers as our competitors are working to steal them.**

The standard, old-school method for driving repeat sales has always
been to seek a new telephone conversation from time to time. Often, that
call is positioned as a means of "checking in" to see how things are going
since the last time they bought something. I think we can do much better
than that, and in Chapter 7 I'll share seven good reasons for having a conversation with your customer that are far better than the tired old "touching
base" cliché.

Today, there are also several digital options for continuing to pour fresh
insights into your clients and lead them to the place where they recognize
they need your help again. Ideally, we want to be able to do that between
telephone calls and conversations if we can. As I said earlier, I truly believe
this represents the greatest opportunity to grow revenue and profitability
for just about any company.

Sequenced Email or Text

In the world of digital selling, a list of opt-in *subscribers* including email
addresses and/or mobile (text) numbers is solid gold. It's literally like
money in the bank. Social followers are great! But you'd be hard-pressed to
find anyone who understands the inner workings of search and social algorithms who didn't agree that an email or text subscriber list is *far* superior.

Social algorithms only show your content to a fraction of the people
who follow you unless you pay for increased exposure. The big social platforms have to make money somehow! However, until an email subscriber
changes their email address, they have basically given you a direct channel
to reach them whenever you want at no charge.

Text messaging is truly the next frontier and the Holy Grail for anyone willing to publish content that subscribers deem worthy of showing
up in their text inbox on a regular basis. The general trends for email read
rates and response rates have been declining in recent years. Meanwhile

the average open rate of a text message currently sits at about 99 percent, with 97 percent of messages being read within 15 minutes of delivery.[2]

If you have not yet begun to build a list of subscribers, start today! Of course, you'll need to serve up something they find valuable enough to stay subscribed to. Otherwise, if you just deluge them with a series of pitches, they will unsubscribe just as fast as they join. In the next chapter, we'll talk extensively about how to build your subscriber list and how to keep them hungry for more.

Podcasts and Live Shows

Perhaps the hottest tool for adding value to a subscriber list, attracting new prospective clients, and turning existing clients into repeat customers is a podcast. Another option is a live show delivered via Facebook, LinkedIn, YouTube, or even a videoconference platform like Webex, Zoom, or GoTo Webinar. This is truly the next level in terms of retaining and serving your follower community.

You can host your show live or prerecord it and release it as a podcast and/or a video on YouTube. You can have guests that add texture and credibility or just share your own insights and ideas. It can be long form, ranging from 20 to 60 minutes, or shorter bites of 3 to 10 minutes.

If you don't enjoy writing but love to talk and tell stories, a podcast or a show might be perfect for you. It seems to fit me like a glove! If you feel you don't possess the expert status you'd like to have just yet, host a podcast with guests that you can interview. One of my favorite approaches is to showcase happy clients who can talk about how you've helped them achieve their goals and objectives.

A podcast or a live or recorded show can add tremendous value to your subscribers and is a spectacular approach to differentiate yourself from competitors. This is a great way to stay atop your customer's or your channel partner's mind and hopefully empower them to recognize they need your help again in the future.

Social Audio

One newer platform for organic social that has tremendous potential is social audio. At the time of this writing, Clubhouse (www.clubhouse.com) is one of the biggest players in this game. Twitter also offers Twitter Spaces, Facebook offers Live Audio Rooms, and LinkedIn is now offering Audio

Rooms for select content creators. An individual user can host their own audio show and invite other users to be part of the audience. It is very easy to allow any audience member to join the discussion, ask questions, make comments, etc.

This can be a very nice platform for retention but can also be quite effective to create new connections. Many people who begin hosting high-quality discussions are able to grow their audience and following very rapidly. And because anyone in the room can raise their hand to take part in the discussion, these kinds of discussion rooms can be a great way to foster many-to-many conversations on any topic imaginable. This is definitely worth exploring for any business owner or corporate salesperson who is willing to initiate and lead a group conversation to build relationships with people who have an interest in any particular topic.

* * *

Before we get into more of the specific tactics of digital selling in the next chapter, let me emphasize this: please don't try to create a digital selling engine that is so complex that it's unsustainable over time. The complexion of your engine needs to be proportional to the amount of time, money, and human resources you can allocate to running it. Starting a podcast that you abandon three months later looks worse than never starting one to begin with. Setting up social profiles on platforms you're not willing to dedicate at least a little time and attention to gives the exact opposite impression from the one you hoped it would.

One social channel that you are willing to invest time in to make new connections is plenty to start with. One great landing page on your website or a sales funnel that is designed to convert web traffic to an email subscriber is awesome for the conversion layer! And starting an email list of even a few hundred people you can keep in touch with weekly or monthly by providing something really valuable to them is a huge accomplishment. Start small. Perfect what you are currently doing and upgrade your engine over time.

Putting These Ideas into Practice

Here are a few action steps to put what's in this chapter to use:

1. *Sketch Out Your Digital Selling Engine*

   Grab a piece of scratch paper and—using the diagram from earlier in this chapter (Figure 4.1) as an example—draw out what your digital selling engine looks like right now. Ask yourself the following questions as they relate to the four layers:

   Connection Layer: What am I currently doing to make new connections—inbound, outbound, or both?

   Conversion Layer: How am I converting connections into something more than just a vague acquaintance or a follower?

   Selling Layer: How am I leveraging digital assets to help do the selling required to obtain a new customer?

   Retention Layer: How am I maintaining contact with my current and past customers to drive retention and repeat sales?

2. *Determine Which Mechanisms Need More of Your Attention Right Now*

   For example, you may have an email subscriber list but haven't invested much energy to continue to nurture those relationships with insight and useful information. You might have a YouTube channel, but haven't done much of anything with it in quite a while.

3. *Decide What Steps You Will Take to Give Your Engine a "Tune-Up"*

   What are three specific actions you could take over the next week or two to improve your engine's efficiency and effectiveness? Maybe it's time to really give your LinkedIn profile a face lift. Or maybe an extreme makeover! Perhaps your company website needs some attention, not only in terms of look and feel, but in what actions your visitors can take to make forward motion in the customer relationship journey.

(continued)

4. *Identify What Additional Piece or Pieces You Might Want to Add at This Time or in the Near Future*

Maybe it's time to start a new email subscriber list and a weekly or monthly newsletter? Set a date for getting it up and running. Or, consider starting your own online show. Just remember, you don't have to commit to three-episodes a week for the rest of your life just yet. Maybe just host a few YouTube Live streams and get a feel for it.

Explore the possibilities and give yourself a chance to see how things work and how your viewers respond before you fully dedicate yourself to any one format. Chances are there will soon be new platforms and options available that don't even exist yet.

CHAPTER 5

Building e-Relationships Throughout the Digital Buying Journey

Now that we've looked at many of the platforms and mediums we might employ as part of our overall digital selling strategy, let's dig into how we use these platforms and tools to advance our relationship with our prospective customers over time. Let's explore how to lead people through what I call the *customer relationship journey.*

To illustrate how powerful it can be to leverage inbound and outbound into a cohesive strategy, I'll share a quick story with you about how a combination of these two approaches can enable you to build e-relationships with your prospects before, during, and after any personal interaction with you.

About a year ago I was chatting with a business owner I know about how to clean up his aging contact list by getting updated email addresses for the people who've changed jobs in recent years. He ended up finding an online service called Seamless.AI (which I mentioned in the previous chapter) to obtain current email addresses and even add landline and mobile telephone numbers for most of those contacts. Way cool! That was my first exposure to Seamless. But over the coming months, it was as if I started seeing Seamless everywhere I looked.

I started noticing posts on LinkedIn talking about how sales pros and marketers can leverage Seamless, most of which featured founder and CEO Brandon Bornancin. Naturally, I took a look at his LinkedIn profile, read all about his incredible serial success as a young entrepreneur, and instantly became a follower and an avid fan.

Some months later I saw an online offer on Facebook to download a free guide on cold-calling from Seamless. I gladly exchanged my contact information for it. As you might imagine, I soon received an email and then a telephone call from an SDR (sales development rep) who helped me understand the overall promise of what Seamless could do for my business. I didn't bite.

A month or two later I happened to notice Brandon's book, *Seven Figure Social Selling*, on Amazon.com and ordered it. It's a great book that's chock-full of examples of exactly what to say on the phone and write in your prospecting emails in hundreds of different sales scenarios. Get a copy!

Then, I stumbled across a couple of really useful videos Brandon shot and posted on YouTube, so I subscribed to his YouTube channel. A few weeks later I got another call from the same SDR, agreed to see a demo from his AE (account executive), loved what I saw in the product, and still didn't buy.

I continued to appreciate the new YouTube videos as they were released as well as regular emails containing helpful prospecting tips that I received as a subscriber to the Seamless email list. A couple of months later, when we decided to double down on our outbound prospecting at my company, we realized that we needed to clean up and expand our prospect lists. I immediately called back the AE with whom I had previously built a relationship and signed up for a yearly subscription with glee.

It took several months for me to walk through that journey, but I never once looked in the direction of a competitor. I even avoided numerous cold calls and emails from other companies along the way. Brandon and his team had built a relationship with me. I didn't want to look around!

After receiving the free guide and free tips via email and on YouTube, meeting a couple of different Seamless employees, and buying the book, I was already a customer. I just hadn't handed over my credit card for the full product yet. It was the combination of the digital assets as well as the persistence of the SDR and the connection I had made with the AE that brought me back when the timing was right.

Interestingly enough, I decided to approach Brandon to interview him for this book. He graciously accepted my request for a live video meeting, and here's the first thing he said:

"It's great to finally meet you, Bill! I bought your book, *Think Like Your Customer*, back when I was getting started. I still use some of the ideas I learned from your book today!" Is that crazy or what? Here I was blown away by what a masterful job he and his team had done building e-relationships with me, never imagining that I had begun an asynchronous relationship with him more than 10 years earlier and didn't even know it!

As you gathered from this story, Brandon and his team at Seamless employed both inbound and outbound techniques to lead me through my buying process over a period of many months. Their ability to combine these two approaches into a cohesive strategy moved me through the customer relationship journey in a highly effective manner.

One of the most important points of this story is . . .

> **To align with how your customers live and buy today, invest in building e-relationships with people wherever they are in their overall process. Then, be willing to continue to invest as you lead them through the customer relationship journey one step at a time, if needed.**

Every person you encounter, whether you actually interact with them or they just partake of your digital content, falls into one of three categories:

1. A prospective customer right now
2. Someone who may become a prospective customer in the future
3. Someone who could recommend you to a prospective customer at some point

Put yourself and your heart out there on every medium you can find. Start pouring into people's lives. Take all the knowledge you have about improving your customer's world and give it away in every format you can think of. Bless people with your insight and advice. And don't expect anything other than goodwill in return. I'll have much more on this as part of our discussion on building your personal brand in Chapter 6.

Using a combination of inbound and outbound, you can create and maintain contact with a virtually unlimited number of prospects as you foster trust, earn preference, and lead them toward an opportunity where you can serve them and add value to their lives.

The Three Phases of the Customer Relationship Journey

The heart of digital selling is learning to leverage a variety of digital assets throughout the complete customer relationship journey, which I break down into three major phases:

1. **Pre-Conversation Phase:** This is the time when we attract and build e-relationships with prospective customers who are in the early stages of their buying process. Or perhaps when they are nowhere near beginning a buying process yet. It includes any one-way (us-to-them) communication that occurs before any real-time conversation takes place.

2. **Conversation Phase:** This is when we have made contact and begin having person-to-person interactions with our prospective client. This might involve face-to-face, video, telephone, chat, DM, or email conversations. Through this phase we are building personal relationships with our prospective customers. We help them work through their buying process as they actively explore, compare, select, and ultimately commit to buying something.

3. **Post-Conversation Phase:** This is the period when we continue to foster relationships after our customer makes a purchase. Here we want to continue to add even more value to their world and potentially create new opportunities to partner with them. This includes the time after any traditional "sales cycle" when we are no longer actively engaging with the customer around a specific project or sales opportunity.

Of course, if you sell in an environment where you never personally communicate with your customer, then any and all "conversations" would actually be e-conversations. Millions of companies are thriving these days selling strictly online. A lot of customers absolutely love it, and many even prefer it!

To make this overall journey easier to visualize, I created a model to illustrate the three major phases and the steps within each phase that represent a complete customer relationship journey from total *stranger* to all-out *champion* (Figure 5.1). This illustration helps simplify the way we think

Figure 5.1   The Customer Relationship Journey

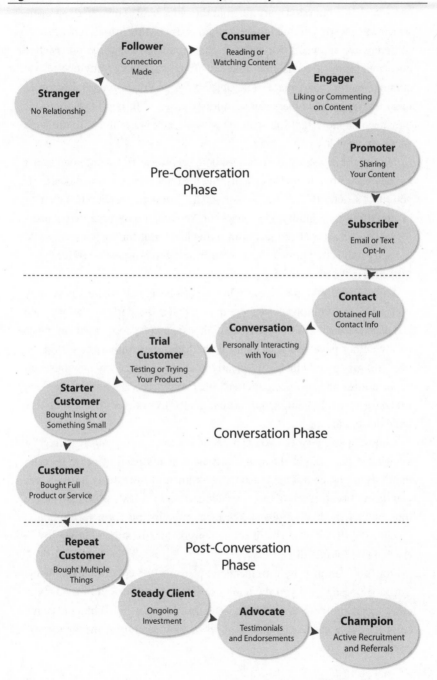

about how to deepen our relationship with our customers over time. As you can see, this is quite a departure from the old school, Three C's approach, which was mostly confined to the second phase of this overall journey.

Today, we can use a variety of digital strategies to engage prospective clients and move the customer relationship forward before any one-to-one communication takes place. The objective is to create a digital environment where our customers can seamlessly progress through these steps as they become more familiar with us, with our company, and with the ways we might be able to serve them.

You might be asking yourself, "Where do I start?" I'd say if you haven't already done so, commit to establishing a strong presence on LinkedIn. If you run a strictly B2C business—or you are promoting a church, a charity, or an online community—Facebook or YouTube could be a better place for you to attract and connect with individuals. But for business networking and establishing professional connections with prospective B2B buyers, LinkedIn is the place to be.

I am blessed with a thriving following on Facebook where I post daily faith-based inspiration and encouragement. It's the perfect platform and audience for that. On any given day, thousands of people read my posts on my author page (www.facebook.com/BillStinnettAuthor) or within the over 100 groups in which I frequently post. But most of my new business opportunities and prospective clients that originate via social come from LinkedIn (www.linkedin.com/in/billstinnett). Connect with me and let's build our brands together!

Choose a space where you can become known as a go-to resource for knowledge and insight that your target customers need at some point in their buying process. One reason I recommend LinkedIn is it also gives you the ability to reach out to your connections via DM, which is—at the time of this writing—probably the most effective platform for outbound prospecting that exists. That is a huge upside for investing your energy in crushing it on LinkedIn.

YouTube can also be a tremendous platform for creating a following. YouTube doesn't give you the ability to interact with or send messages to other members the way LinkedIn does. But because YouTube is a search engine, people can easily find you when they search on the topics you post about.

An old boss of mine gave me a fantastic piece of advice many years ago. He said . . .

> **"You don't have to close a big deal all in one conversation. Just help your customer take the baby steps toward the close."**

Today it sometimes takes a few baby steps to even close someone on agreeing to accept your phone call! Am I right? I often think of this whole process a bit like online dating. Our would-be customers often want to check us out and draw some conclusions about us online before they make a commitment to start any two-way communication.

Many of us who do our best work when talking to customers in real time would rather just skip all these early steps and get right to a live video or telephone conversation. But the quality of our live conversations and the likelihood of converting them to an opportunity improve substantially when we build e-relationships and earn some trust and rapport digitally before we get on the call. When you build e-relationships and engage in e-conversations, you allow your prospects to self-select and choose to move to the next step in the relationship journey on their timetable.

The Pre-Conversation Phase

Now, let's further explore how to advance your relationship with pro-spective customers. We'll start by looking at a progression of steps of the pre-conversation phase that are designed to move prospects from complete strangers to active opt-in email or text subscribers.

1. Stranger: *No Relationship*

A good example of a stranger would be users of a social platform whom we have not yet connected with. They could also be people actively browsing YouTube or Spotify who have yet to subscribe to our channel or podcast.

Of course, you can choose to simply purchase names and contact info of target prospects from a variety of sources and go straight outbound with telephone and email outreach. That's fine if you are planning on calling a high volume of people where you can't take the time to warm things up with an e-relationship before you reach out.

For a more focused approach on a shorter list of targeted prosects, I prefer to attempt to proactively connect or at least communicate with as many as possible on LinkedIn first. One way to start would be to look up a refined target list on LinkedIn Navigator and start just cold-inviting people to connect. Unfortunately, your response rates will range from "OK" to absolutely terrible, which may include being reported for asking to connect to a person you don't already know outside LinkedIn. (Yes, that happens. I've been there.)

To increase your odds of success dramatically, start by looking at the profiles of target prospects and reading some of their recent posts. Add a like or a comment to some of their posts as a first step. Maybe even share one of their posts on your timeline if you think it's good and that your own customers would benefit from it.

You can start a conversation with literally anyone on a social platform, even if you are not "connected" with them, by leaving a comment on their posts. I've been doing this for years. Often, I'll even make mention of something that impressed me about their profile in a comment I leave on a post.

Here's a great suggestion that you can use immediately . . .

> **Learn to use comments on other people's posts as a way to start a dialog the same way you'd mingle at a live networking event. Simply join the conversation your prospect is already having with other people online.**

Social platforms have become a hotbed for predatory sales tactics. LinkedIn is teaming with a zillion people trying to figure out every way possible to coax and cajole people into a "quick 15-minute conversation" the instant they connect. If you've been doing that, stop it! You're burning opportunities to actually build quality e-relationships. Earn the opportunity for a conversation if it makes sense. But start with a legitimate connection first.

Leave some friendly comments for the people you want to meet. Engage with *their* content. Ask them some questions. Show them some love. Almost everyone will eventually acknowledge you. Then you may choose to send a request to connect once they know you are a human being. Also make sure to include a personal note in your connection request. My cutting-edge, top secret format for the personal note is something along the lines of the following:

> *Really enjoyed your post on _____, John. Thanks*
> *for your kind reply to my comment. Are you open to new*
> *connections on LinkedIn?*

Keep it simple and keep it real!

To illustrate just how powerful this approach of starting conversations as comments on social posts can be, have a look at the executive endorsements printed on the back cover and just inside the front cover of this book. Many of those relationships—which have led to major training and consulting projects with some of the largest companies and most high-ranking sales executives in the world—began as conversations I initiated within the comments section of their LinkedIn posts long before I ever had a first-level connection with them. This *works*!

2. Follower: *Connection Made*

Followers could be a connection on a social platform or a subscriber to a blog, podcast, or YouTube channel. Growing your follower base is a foundational element of any digital attraction strategy. Whether you've just registered a new social profile or already have some connections, you'll want to start sending new requests to connect, as appropriate.

In every workshop I do on this topic, I make this same suggestion . . .

Make it a habit of requesting to connect on LinkedIn with *every person* you meet in a business setting!

I am stunned how many people will not put in the effort to do this. For years I have endeavored to connect with everyone I meet, if possible. That has resulted in tens of thousands of connections. At this point, I truly believe that if I never met another person, I already have enough LinkedIn connections to find all the work I would ever need for the rest of my life. You can do that too!

Many of those connections are people who have attended one or more of my classroom or online workshops. So they're actually more than just followers. They are my friends! If you haven't yet done this, make a commitment to get it done in the next 30 days and stay current with it for the rest of your career. Connect with every single contact you have, every name in your CRM system, and every old business card sitting in a drawer someplace. That alone will open up a whole new world from which to grow.

Social platforms are constantly presenting you with "People You May Know" suggestions. Many of them have interests or connections in common with you and would likely agree to connect with you. But you might want to start by simply following them and making comments on their posts to begin with. Joining LinkedIn or Facebook groups of like-minded people can also be a great way to find those who have similar interests and backgrounds.

By default, every person you connect with on a social platform becomes a follower. But users are becoming more and more leery about connecting with strangers. Both LinkedIn and Facebook have cracked down on the practice of inviting mass quantities of people to connect and have instituted daily limits. The platform will also track acceptance rates. If you are approaching a lot of strangers to connect and getting low response rates, your account may be flagged, and the organic reach of your posts can suffer.

Of course, to cast a wider net and increase the chances of attracting and connecting with more followers who may one day become your customers, you have to publish content worth following. Read on!

3. Consumer: *Reading, Watching, or Listening to Content*

As a consumer, a person would partake of the insights and ideas you are making available to them through social media posts, blogs, articles, YouTube videos, or whatever other platforms you are leveraging. Social platforms often report how many views or impressions a post receives. But a "view" can be as little as a simple *scroll by*. That might qualify as an "impression," but until people actually stop scrolling and read or listen to your insights, you're not really changing hearts and minds.

Converting followers into consumers of what you publish is all about the quality and presentation of the content you post. As we've already discussed, people don't follow you to see ads. They follow you to learn, to be informed, or to be entertained. Social media is the new TV. You can be known as someone who pummels them with "commercials," or you can be the one who makes their day better, more interesting, more enriching, and maybe even more fun.

Take a close look at the content that does well (gets a lot of engagement and exposure) on whatever platform you are using to build a following. What are the characteristics of that content? Is it text only, text with images, images only, or video? All of these can be effective for different reasons.

Images get people to stop scrolling long enough to see what you have to say with your written content. Avoid stock imagery or anything that looks like advertisement. The images that draw people in, interestingly enough, are photos of yourself or snapshots with you and your colleagues. These pictures tend to make the post more personal and less "corporate." An image is also great for a very short message superimposed over a compelling photo or graphic design.

This is important: when posting text, with or without images or video, always space your text with a blank line between sentences. This makes it infinitely more readable! But just as importantly, it makes your post twice as long as the single-spaced paragraph structure you learned in school. Algorithms track and love both "dwell time" (i.e., how long someone sits on your content) and the amount of time users spend scrolling on a single piece of content. So the longer the better, as long as it's engaging.

The opening line of your post needs to be as compelling as possible. Some experts recommend polarizing statements, such as "Everything you thought you knew about _____ is wrong!" Or "Your _____ is costing you customers and profit." Other good concepts for opening lines include, "Would you like to know how to _____ ?" and, "Here's a lesson I learned the hard way . . ." Much like the subject line of an email, the first sentence of your post needs to be interesting enough to get people to click on "See more."

Video posts can be very compelling and engaging when done well. Quick tips: if you are using your phone, get a stand or a tripod so you can move it away from your face a bit more than just arm's length. A huge face in the frame is not very appealing in a social post. Start smiling before you begin speaking, and for heaven's sake, trim the first second or two of dead footage off the video before posting it. Nothing looks phonier than starting out with a blank, confused demeanor (as if you're trying to figure out how to get your camera turned on) and suddenly becoming all excited and bubbly once you realize the video is rolling. (Eye-roll)

Video will typically get significantly less social "reach" than straight text. Which simply means fewer people will see it. But video does produce higher engagement rates and, I find, much higher conversion rates in terms of profile views and inquiries. One approach is to mix media by releasing some posts in straight text, some with images, and some video. Many popular creators have had success by establishing a signature format and "look and feel" that they use all the time. This produces a consistent experience and makes their content immediately recognizable to their fans.

For my inspirational posts on Facebook, I use the same style background every morning. Loyal fans tell me they open the app while drinking their coffee and start scrolling, looking for that familiar look and feel of my posts. I do the same thing whenever I post videos on LinkedIn.

You don't have to spend a lot of money to start using video effectively. A smartphone and a simple stand or tripod is fine. But upgrade to a higher quality external microphone if you can. The quality of the audio can make a huge difference in how compelling your video will be.

If you want to take video for social more seriously, a DSLR camera will take your game up several notches. You can also start editing your video and adding images and motion graphics when you are ready. If you want some suggestions on producing great video for social media, you can download a free guide I created called *7 Ways to Make Your Social Videos Absolutely Outstanding* at: www.salesexcellence.com/handbook.

Here's the main message that I'd like to convey . . .

If you want people to consume your content, you have to give them something more interesting and compelling than the three zillion other posts in their feed. And you have to do it *extremely* consistently!

What many people getting started with social don't realize is that your posts are never seen by the majority of your followers. Most consumers (viewers) probably have hundreds or, more likely, thousands of connections. They'll never scroll far enough to see everybody's content. Social media algorithms determine the priority of what is displayed at the top of their feed, so the average user sees only a tiny fraction of the material posted by everyone they follow.

Social algorithms are designed to serve up content that the user is most likely to be interested in and engage with. Naturally, they're going to prioritize a new post from the same person whose post you liked or commented on yesterday. Have you noticed how you see content from the same two dozen people every single day? Chances are those are people who post every day. And when you stop to read or engage with their content in some way, you're likely to see their post again tomorrow. The converse is also true. If you never engage with people's content, the algorithm will soon stop showing you their posts.

Likewise, when you put a barrage of ads or boring and unoriginal content in front of your followers, they won't engage either. Once the algorithm stops showing them your content, it can be next to impossible to ever get back to the top of their feed. They are still followers; they just don't *see* you anymore. So there is an element of "care and feeding" required to retain the followers that you worked so hard to get in the first place. This is why quality and consistency are so crucial!

Keep in mind that at the end of the day, what matters is not how many total followers you have on social media. What really matters is how many people actively consume what you post and what epiphany occurred or what new conclusion they reached when they read or watched it. The name of the game is changing hearts, changing minds, and inspiring people to take some kind of action.

4. Engager: *Liking or Commenting on Your Content*

Most people who post on social media cannot resist tracking the number of likes or comments their posts produce. It's the ultimate in social *gamification*, like keeping a tally of how many points you score in your favorite video game. To be completely transparent, I find it absolutely addicting.

That's why it's so important to remember . . .

The goal of using social media for digital selling is *not* engagement in your posts. The goal is conversion from one stage to the next in the customer relationship journey!

Likes and comments don't pay the bills! That being said, they do indicate that what you're putting out to the world is resonating with people. Social *engagement*, as it is called, is what the platform algorithms use to determine whether or not to push your content out to more followers and viewers. Engagement determines reach! If you want more people to see your stuff, you have to get people to engage with it.

Engagement also provides social proof to everyone who sees your content that people support or endorse what you are posting. It can actually be a major factor in the overall impression you make on your followers. Whether it's true or not, when people see a post with a lot of engagement, they perceive it to be more credible and worthy of attention and consumption.

Our aim should be to produce the most stimulating and electrifying content and insight available *anywhere*. But even the world's most valuable and powerful insights are worthless if they never get into the hands of people who can appreciate them and do something with them. If your customers— past, present, and future—don't see you or hear from you, it won't be long before they find someone else to pay attention to.

Great social content that *speaks to* people should be designed with one of these four objectives in mind:

Instruct: Teach people how to do something, how to avoid something, how to fix something, or how to accomplish something.

Enlighten: Inform people and make them aware of some new trend, some new bit of knowledge, a new threat coming their way, or a new opportunity available to them.

Inspire: Provide encouragement to help people believe in themselves and what's possible as well as the motivation to do something about it.

Entertain: Make people laugh, bring a smile to their face, or just give them a temporary escape from the tedious, the stressful, or the mundane.

Advertisements that basically say, "Here's my product. Call me!" receive very little engagement. Ads simply don't *move* people. For someone to muster up the energy to smash the like button or go to all the trouble of typing a comment, they have to conclude more than just, "I like this." They have to feel compelled to tell the author and the rest of the world, "This matters to me," "I identify with this," or "Everybody needs to see this!"

Here are a few concepts for social posts that tend to drive a lot of engagement:

- Give a shout-out to a coworker who helped you.
- Publicly thank or brag about your customers.
- Share a lesson you learned the hard way.
- Talk about a personal setback, express gratitude for overcoming it, and give credit to whoever helped you.
- Share some insight as if you were giving a keynote presentation.
- Answer one or more frequently asked questions.
- Share some observation you (or your company) have made about an industry trend that would help your customer take advantage of an opportunity or avoid making a mistake.
- Provide six keys to do something that a lot of people want to do.
- Share the findings of someone else's research and tag them in the post. They will love you!

Stories that followers can relate to and identify with are very compelling. People love to show support when they can see themselves reflected in what they read or watch. These kinds of posts can really drive engagement, but make sure as many of your posts as possible contain highly substantive content related to solving your customers' problems and helping them make buying decisions as well.

It's important to show your human side. Share your personality. But make sure everything isn't all about you. There is little business value in amassing a huge following if you're not also helping at least some of your followers move upward through the pyramid of awareness toward becoming a qualified prospect.

Social algorithms tend to punish content that is designed to manipulate readers or viewers with phrases like "please like my post" or "leave a comment" in the body of a post. However, there are a number of questions that you can ask at the end of your posts that tend to trigger likes and comments. Once you read this list, you'll start noticing these at the end of many people's posted content. Here are some of my favorites:

- Agreed?
- Thoughts?
- Suggestions?
- Anything else?
- What did I miss?
- What would you add?
- What's been your experience?
- Would love to hear your opinion . . .

Social platforms are also very sensitive to any content placed in a post that would take users away from their platform. If you put a link to your website in the body of a post, it will likely get very limited reach. One of the techniques that is widely used is to place links, hashtags, and any kind of self-promotion in the comments section on an original post. If you want to provide a link, you can add a note in the body of your post saying, "Link in first comment below." This will make an incredible difference in the reach of the post.

Many creators now regularly place a little pitch in the comments section of their posts inviting people to a free webinar or providing a link to a You-Tube video or some other special offer. A very recent trend is for creators to add a comment to their own post saying, "Please like this comment and leave a comment of your own and I'll send you a free _____." These trends are constantly changing, so just watch the most popular creators and copy what they are doing.

We all tend to be impressed when we see people with 100,000 or 500,000 social followers. But a much better indicator of their social media presence is the number of people who regularly engage with their content. My daily posts on my Facebook author page consistently get more engagement than some creators who have a million followers.

The *ultimate* way to measure the success of a social media strategy, however, is by the action that readers take after they see a post. This is impossible to determine just by looking at the post or the user profile. I've had many posts that received less than 100 likes produce a lead that turned into a $50,000 or $100,000 project!

I love it when I get a call or a DM from someone whom I haven't spoken to in years saying, "I loved your post today. We've got a new sales team that needs training on exactly what you were talking about." Cha-ching! But here's an interesting note: almost without exception, the person who makes that call or sends that message never actually pushed the like button or commented on the post. Go figure!

5. Promoter: *Sharing Your Content*

When people so identify with your content that they are willing to repost it on their own timeline, it represents the ultimate endorsement. In essence, they are saying to all of their followers, "Do you see this? I identify with this. I support this and I want you to hear about it, too." Sharing drives your organic reach like crazy. For this reason, I like to make sure people know they have permission to share my posts.

If you say, "Please share my post," the algorithm will read that and it will probably negatively impact your reach. I have had pretty good success simply saying, "Share as you see fit." My favorite technique is placing a tiny bit of text embedded into the .jpeg image on my inspirational posts for Facebook saying, "Feel free to share." But keep in mind that all the social platforms now scan your images and use optical character recognition to detect any text displayed in the image. Consequently, anything you embed in your images will be read by the algorithm.

One of the strangest things about social algorithms is that they boost your content significantly when other people share it with their followers. However, the reach and exposure of shared content for the person who shares it is absolutely terrible! Because of this, one huge mistake you can easily make when trying to grow your reach on either LinkedIn or Facebook is simply reposting or sharing other people's posts. There's nothing necessarily *wrong* with doing it. The original author will probably be thrilled. But the platforms, especially LinkedIn, strongly favor original content. Look at the recent posts of someone who primarily shares reposts of other people's content. The reach of those posts is usually very limited, and they receive very limited engagement.

I'm familiar with one LinkedIn member who has over 200,000 followers and posts several times a day. But because he shares other people's posts and hyperlinks to off-site articles almost exclusively, he's lucky if he sees 20 engagements on a post. That means 199,980 of his followers didn't engage and 198,000 of them probably haven't even seen one of his reposts in years. Someone with only 3,000 highly engaged followers who consistently posts engaging original content would likely have far more organic reach and influence than he does.

One of the best techniques I've ever learned for sharing content and strengthening e-relationships is to take a few good points from someone else's article or a post I read and then write my own original post about how much I loved the article. If you decide to use this technique, share the three main things you took away from the article, tag the original author in your post, and even place the link to the original article as a comment and add a note in the body of your post saying, "Link to article in comments below."

This is a fantastic way to do several things all at the same time:

- Provide great content to your followers.
- Score major points with the original author because you share their content and extend *their* reach.
- Get your post in front of *their* followers since you tagged them in your post.
- Keep the algorithms happy.

. . . all at the same time!

6. Subscriber: *Email or Text Opt-in*

The email or text opt-in subscriber stage is one of the most important steps your customers can take in the relationship journey. They are basically signing up to hear from you whenever you have something new to share. People can subscribe to a blog, a YouTube channel, a podcast, or some form of email correspondence such as a weekly newsletter.

Social followers are awesome! But, as I mentioned before, typically only a small fraction of your followers will ever see your content. Ironically, the larger your following, the smaller the percentage of your followers will see what you post. As I explained in the previous chapter, email subscribers are far more valuable. Once someone has opted in to hear from you via email or text, you don't have to try to outsmart the algorithms and constantly compete with every other content creator for placement in the feed.

Much of the content and insights we want to share with our audience should be posted publicly for all to see. But it's also fine to hold some of it back to be shared only after a relationship has advanced to a stage where it makes sense to offer your best guidance and advice.

I save my very best material for those who are paying customers, of course. But I also freely share *some* of my stuff with prospects who agree to join me on a videoconference. I think of it as sort of an exchange: my ideas for their willingness to have a conversation about how we might use those ideas to improve their business. I also regularly create special articles, sales tools, checklists, and free guides to share with people as *gated content*.

The idea of gated content is creating some kind of *gate* that a person has to pass through to gain access to it. The practice of trading a free white paper, a free guide, or a free online course in exchange for your prospect's contact info has been in use for decades, so this may not be the first time you've ever heard of this. But the question isn't are you familiar with the practice. The question is, "Are you *using* gated content to convert your social followers to email or text subscribers?" If not, maybe it's time to get started!

I use gated content on LinkedIn and other platforms constantly to grow my email subscriber list. My favorite way to leverage it is with a short video post sharing one tip from a special article, checklist, or a free mini-workshop I am offering. After I share some insight or a helpful tip, I usually say something like this:

> *If you'd like a copy, just leave a comment below and I'll DM you the link to download it.*

This approach accomplishes several things at the same time:

- I provide one valuable tip for free (generosity).
- My offer generates comments like crazy, which drives the reach of the post dramatically.

- If I get a comment from someone I'm not yet connected with, it's the perfect reason to reply, asking that *they send me* a request to connect so I can DM them the link. Note: it's key to ask them to invite you as opposed to you inviting them so you don't hit the daily invitation limits.

- Every person who follows the link I send them via DM can subscribe to my mailing list by entering a name and email address to get access to the free content.

- I send them other free tools whenever I release them.

Here's an example of how effective this can be. I wrote an article in 2019 called *7 Good Reasons for Having a Conversation with Your Customer*, which I offer as free gated content every four to six months on LinkedIn. Literally thousands of people have subscribed to our free tools mailing list (see www.salesexcellence.com/handbook) over the years as a result of regularly offering that one piece of gated content alone! I typically offer one new tool like this every month.

If you are a salesperson for a large corporation and you don't have a website, blog, or newsletter of your own, you can certainly still leverage the idea of gated content as outlined here. Your marketing team probably already has plenty of valuable assets you can use, a landing page to which to drive traffic, and a mailing list people can subscribe to. Go partner with them! Put all those tools your marketing department already has to good use. They will love you for it!

The Conversation Phase

The purpose of all your efforts in the pre-conversation phase is to earn enough trust and rapport with your followers that those who need your help will either contact you or provide their contact information to you. Once you establish this connection, you can continue to communicate with them while you build rapport and preference. If you decide to incorporate outbound into your overall strategy, you're now ready to start your outreach, when you think the time is right. Ideally, you've already had some interaction with at least some of these subscribers via comments and replies to social posts.

7. Contact: *They Provide Full Contact Info*

For this discussion, we'll define a contact as someone for whom we have complete contact information, including full name, company name, title, email address, phone number, and ideally even a mobile number. A mobile phone number is surely the most coveted and powerful bit of contact info for today's digital seller.

When people provide their information in exchange for something of value, such as the kinds of digital assets we've talked about, there is an implied expectation that someone's going to contact them at some point. You'll have to determine what you are comfortable with when it comes to outreach. I'm of the opinion that reaching out to someone once we've established an e-relationship and engaged in some form of e-conversation is a next logical step! Inbound purists will disagree, of course.

Many outbounders subscribe to the "pick up the darn phone and call them right now" school of thought. If I'm already connected to them on LinkedIn, I actually favor scheduling an appointment for the conversation by sending a 60-second video or audio message via the LinkedIn smartphone app as opposed to just surprising them over the telephone. I simply prefer to invest my live-conversation time with prospects that have already heard from me and have elected to join a call.

Sometimes, I use the short video to simply let my prospect know I'll be calling them at 2:45 the following day as opposed to asking *permission* to call. I'm also having success sending a meeting invitation to people that includes a link to a short, custom video—which I shot just for them—explaining why they would find value in taking my call. I also let them know that they can reply with a suggestion of a different time if my proposed time doesn't work for them. I'll have much more on digital prospecting in Chapter 7.

8. Conversation: *Personally Interacting with You*

For any of us who grew up in the world of synchronous selling, a "conversation" is synonymous with a meeting, videoconference, or telephone call. But with today's digital communication capabilities, there are a number of innovative options. One that is gaining incredible traction is live chat with people who have come to visit your website. This is a fantastic option to give visitors the ability to ask questions in real time without having to talk to you in person.

Companies like Drift (www.drift.com) and others are truly changing the game by offering "conversational marketing" tools that enable customers to literally converse with a salesperson entirely digitally while maintaining control of the communication and even protecting their own anonymity. Definitely check out the Drift website for a visit to the future of enterprise-class virtual selling! Likewise, anyone with a website can install a simple and very inexpensive plugin app such as LiveChat (www.livechat.com) and not only be notified every time a new person arrives on their site but hold live chat conversations with visitors through a free smartphone app. Amazing!

Since we installed LiveChat on our website (www.salesexcellence.com), the number of inquiries (i.e., conversions) nearly doubled. Additionally, we've been able to start conversations with visitors immediately, while they are still on the site, instead of minutes or even hours later. Almost no one opts to use the antiquated "Contact Us" form anymore. Simple but powerful technologies are creating opportunities to have digital conversations in ways that were never before possible.

But even with all the cool tech, let's not forget the importance of a good old-fashioned telephone conversation. In the story I told at the beginning of this chapter, the consistent outreach from the Seamless SDR was a critical element of me moving forward through my customer journey—as was the live product demonstration and relationship I developed with the AE over live video.

As far as building relationships and persuasion are concerned, whenever we can engage with people one-to-one in real time, it beats asynchronous selling any day. But in the Seamless story I shared at the beginning of this chapter, it was many of those asynchronous digital touches that kept me loyal, actively engaged, and progressing toward becoming a customer in between those conversations with a real person.

9. Trial Customer: *Testing or Trying Your Product or Service*

In situations where it's possible, offering your customers a free trial of your product or service is one of the very best ways to advance the relationship beyond the conversation stage with little or no risk to them. By now, *all* of us have surely signed up for some type of an online service that offers a 30-day free trial. Sometimes companies make you enter your credit card and cancel within 30 days if you want out. Sometimes no credit card is required.

Here's my suggestion . . .

Regardless of what you offer, you should come up with one or maybe a half dozen ways that your customers can try you out before they buy.

Here are some examples:

- Free assessment with reported results
- Free consultation
- Limited time access (14 or 30 days)
- First visit free
- Loaner system
- Purchase with a right to return
- Cancel anytime. Pay only the installation fee.

However, I frequently suggest requiring some kind of commitment from the buyer in proportion to what it costs you to provide the trial. If your fulfillment costs are next to nothing, you don't have much to lose. But if it's going to require hard costs, capital outlay, or someone's time, I want the customer to have skin in the game. The best free trials require the customer to actually take them seriously and be prepared to move forward with a purchase if the trial goes well.

The aim here is to advance the customer journey to a stage where the perspective client starts consuming or partaking of the payback our product or service delivers. Ideally, they can even start to see and measure the results! Providing your customer with some sort of trial to experience what it's like to be your customer is a vital component of the overall customer journey, and today's technology makes this possible now more than ever.

10. Starter Customer: *Bought Insight or Something Small*

One outstanding strategy that is gaining momentum for advancing relationships is giving people the opportunity to become what I call a "starter customer," thus moving them one step closer to being a full customer. The psychology behind this is that an individual or a company might be willing to invest a little money with you even if they are not quite ready to invest a lot.

Applying this strategy may not fall solely under the responsibility of sales and marketing. An element of product development could be required. The idea is to create some kind of an inexpensive offering that represents a small commitment for your prospective customer so they can get a taste of what it might be like to work with you. It's another baby step your customer can take on the way to buying your full product or service. Some marketers call this a "mini-offer" or a "micro-offer."

Here are some examples of a mini-offer:

- Paid needs assessments
- Paid feasibility assessment
- Paid product trial
- Limited consulting engagement
- Three-month discounted membership
- Pilot engagement

Examples of a micro-offer could be information and insight that you can deliver entirely online or hands-off, such as these:

- Book or e-book
- How-to guide
- Results of polls or surveys
- Access to special research or reports
- Online courses

I especially like these kinds of marketable assets because they . . .

1. Give your buyers a chance to experience being your customer. Once they spend a little money with you, spending more is less of a psychological hurdle.

2. Provide substantial value and insight that can further sell the value you can provide and propel your customer through their buying process.

3. Offer a way to differentiate yourself from any competitor who doesn't provide this kind of guidance and advice.

To come up with ideas for mini-offers or micro-offers that you can use to create starter customers, think about "unbundling" your comprehensive offering. Of course, there is a risk that your mini-offer could cannibalize or negatively impact the sales of your full product. This is why I often recommend starting out by simply offering some of your *advice*, as a micro-offer, at an affordable price and not necessarily offering a significant portion of your normal deliverables. This can give you a chance to demonstrate your expertise as you enable your customer to come to know, like, and trust you even more.

The best micro-offers will help your clients conclude that they need your full product. Today, many of our corporate engagements come as a result of someone buying one of our online courses to use as a test drive. If they see the quality of one module—and the impact it can have on the thinking and sales behavior of the learner—they are much more likely to take the next step toward a larger investment.

One of my favorite stories to tell about using the "starter customer" concept involves one of my very first engagements with a Fortune 500 company back in 2002. My prospective client liked me (it seemed), and they liked the overview of the training program I had custom-tailored for them. But they were still concerned about hiring an unknown one-man shop to train their enterprise sales team. I said, "If you pay for my travel expenses, I'll come and do a pilot workshop for you. If you don't love it, there will be no additional charge. But if you *do* love it, I'll invoice you for my usual fee."

All they were really committing to was the travel expenses. As I suspected, once they saw the complete program—which I had built based on their expressed needs and to their specifications—they were absolutely thrilled. They not only happily paid the full fee for the pilot but then proceeded to send me to over 20 cities on four continents to train their entire global sales team.

11. Customer: *Bought Full Product or Service*

If my hunch is right, I don't need to explain what a paying customer is. Nor do I need to convince you that becoming a paying customer is a step you want to help as many people take as possible. The most important point I want to make here is that it is just too easy—once we get a signed contract and receive payment—to emotionally disengage and start looking for the next one. This is probably the biggest mistake we can make, but we are all guilty of this, at least once in a while.

Don't forget that there is an entire third phase of the customer relationship journey *after* someone becomes a paying customer. Let's not disappear on them the instant the ink dries on the contract. This last phase is where the real value of the customer relationship starts to emerge and the big returns on our investment of time and energy are found.

Let me emphasize that throughout the conversation phase, and especially once someone becomes a paying customer, make it a point to establish a connection with them via every communication channel you can. Make sure you have all their telephone numbers. Connect with them on LinkedIn—and maybe even on WhatsApp and Slack, if appropriate—so you can keep in touch with them even if they change companies. Most of all, come up with a reason to initiate correspondence via text message. Get into their contact list on their smartphone and get them into yours. Once you have a text connection, you've got a hotline that can be strategically used to reach people even when they don't have the time or the bandwidth to respond to your phone calls or emails.

The Post-Conversation Phase

Once your customer completes a purchase or an investment—meaning they buy something and you deliver what you've promised—we enter what I refer to as the post-conversation phase. Sadly, taking care of customers and fostering repeat business often becomes a time management challenge. We wrestle with the question, "How do I balance the time it takes to keep in touch with my current clients while trying to land new ones?"

One of the best ways to literally multiply your time is to use digital assets to keep moving your client relationships forward even when you can't be there. Now let's look at the four remaining stages of the overall customer relationship journey.

12. Repeat Customer: *Bought Multiple Things*

In earlier chapters, we talked extensively about treating our existing clients like brand-new clients. Ideally, we would frequently reengage to figure out where they are now and where they want to go next. But we can also use digital communication to literally help them recognize the problems they are encountering in their current state and envision a compelling desired future state.

Start using your opt-in email subscriber list and your social media accounts to do more than just advertise "special offers" and limited time "discounts." Educate and inform people with both short-form and long-form content that either *helps* them right now and/or prepares them for the future. Try creating assets on topics such as these:

How to Get the Most out of Your Investment in _____ (what you sell)

4 Impending Threats for the Future of the _____ Industry

3 Alarming Trends in the _____ Industry That Every Company Must Prepare For

5 Secrets That Leading Hospitals Are Using to Minimize Theft by Employees

6 Ways to Keep Your Best Sales Talent from Being Poached by Your Competitors

Of course, you'll end up mentioning new solutions you are bringing to market. You'll also probably showcase your full stack of products and services as a means of making your clients aware of all the ways you can help them. But you'll do it within the context of empowering them and equipping them to overcome the challenges they face in the present and achieve their goals and objectives going forward.

These kinds of insights could, of course, take the form of an article or a text-based post. But I want to encourage you to explore shooting video that you can include in an email, within your social posts, or upload to YouTube. Once you have a relationship established—such as you would have with someone who has bought from you before—a video is a much more powerful way to keep yourself top-of-mind. It's much more engaging and helps maintain the feeling of familiarity and the rapport much better than written words alone.

13. Steady Client: *Ongoing Investment*

For some of us, there is a stage beyond repeat customer that we'll call the "steady client" stage. Depending on the solutions you provide, perhaps you already offer a product or a service that your customer can commit to on an ongoing basis. Maybe it's a yearlong contract instead of doing one-off projects. Maybe it's a service agreement instead of only providing repairs on a "break/fix" basis.

In many industries, creative companies have recognized and devised ways to continue to bring value to customers on a regular basis as opposed to only when a new perceived problem arises. How could you support and empower your customer beyond Point B (the transaction) and help ensure they actually arrive at Point C and achieve their desired results consistently over time?

As with the mini-offers and micro-offers mentioned earlier, this has as much to do with product development as it does with digital selling. But often this kind of ongoing service and support can be delivered via some digital mechanism such as an online help desk, real-time chat support, electronic reminders, remote monitoring, etc.

Our business completely changed in 2012 when we started offering online training and coaching reinforcement to go along with our classroom workshops. The size of our average client engagement doubled overnight. And our clients received far *more* than double the value!

Figure out what your company already offers or can offer in this regard, and endeavor to enroll every customer possible in some form of ongoing service agreement, support plan, subscription, or retainer. There's no better way to continue to pour into the customer partnership on a daily or weekly basis.

14. Advocate: *Testimonials and Endorsements*

Advocates are clients who are willing to testify on your behalf and tell the world how you've helped them. I can count on one hand (or maybe two) the number of companies I've ever worked with who've even scratched the surface of what is possible in terms of gathering and leveraging customer testimonials. This is an area where my company could improve, too!

Are we so crazy busy trying to find the next client that we don't have time to assess and document the success and the results we've already helped our existing clients achieve? Here are two reasons why it's so important for us to collect and leverage customer success stories.

The first is that a large percentage of the time, the effort to assess the value you've already delivered naturally leads to a conversation about how to expand the partnership even further. And second, documenting what you've already helped your current customers achieve can be turned into one of the best tools you could possibly have to attract and influence new customers!

Go back to every customer who's willing to have a conversation and ask them if they've benefited from the relationship. Nothing builds your own confidence quite like hearing your customer telling you how good you are! And if there is some aspect of the relationship that they're not happy with, at least you'll know about it and have the opportunity to do something about it!

Once you have some evidence, write up a story about it and put it on your website. Shoot a video of your customer telling their own success story and post it on YouTube. Make a new post on LinkedIn talking about your mutually beneficial relationship, including a testimonial quote. You'll get some virtually priceless exposure, and they will too!

In a world where anyone located anywhere can put up a website and call themselves the global leader in _____ (fill in the blank), nothing speaks louder than a real client talking about how you added measurable value to their world.

What format should a success story take? Here's a simple but powerful outline based on the customer results model from 'Chapter 2:

1. **Their Point A:** The current state your customer was in when you found them, including the negative consequences surrounding it. Whenever possible, quantify those consequences in terms of one or more units of measure, such as dollars lost, hours or days wasted, number of customers lost, etc.

2. **Their Point C:** The outcomes and results your customer wanted to achieve at their desired future state. Again, quantify with a unit measure such as goals they had around increasing revenue or throughput, reducing downtime, or minimizing customer churn, etc.

3. **Your B:** The product and/or service solution you provided to help them get from A to C.

4. **Their Outcomes and Results:** The tangible and measurable improvements they saw expressed in units of measure over a specific period of time. *And*—here is the really important part—how those outcomes impacted your customer *personally.*

I know of no other undertaking more important in the world of digital selling than documenting your clients' successes and making those stories available online. Do something on this before this week is over!

15. Champion: *Actively Recruiting and Referring Clients to You*

The ultimate destination of the customer relationship journey is creating champions who will not only say a few nice things about you when asked, but will promote you and tell other people every chance they get. How do you do this? My approach has always been to literally join their team. I align myself with every major stakeholder I'm able to gain access to, understand their goals and objectives, and do everything I can to help them achieve those goals and objectives.

I recommend that sellers who want to build a real partnership should adopt their clients' business philosophy and embrace their mission statement. Literally "go to work" for them! As one of my happy clients put it: "Sales Excellence literally became an extension of our own internal team." That's the goal!

You can, of course, simply ask clients to keep you in mind and to recommend you whenever they find the opportunity. But using the approach I just outlined, I've found that I seldom have to ask. When I become their champion, they somehow naturally become mine, too.

Here's the next step: regularly equip your happy clients with insight and knowledge that is not only helpful for them but is packaged up so it's easy to share with their friends. Create digital assets that are easily sharable, such as:

- A one-pager covering how you can help solve three major customer problems with your new _____ (fill in the blank) solution.

- A research report showing how much _____ (time or money) you helped your average client save last year using your _____ (fill in the blank) solution.

- A series of YouTube videos each talking about a specific business outcome you and your company can help your clients achieve.

You can include these in an automated email sequence you send to a mailing list of existing clients. But I like to send a personal message—my preference is DM or text—to my best clients every so often thanking them for their business and for helping let others know about how we've partnered together.

Before I attach anything, I like to ask, "Do you mind if I send you a document (or a link to something) we just released that you can pass along to anyone you think might like to see it?" Your strong supporters will be thrilled to look at it and forward it to others, as appropriate. People frequently DM me back saying, "Hey I just passed your one-pager on to the so-and-so manager in the other department. Here's her contact info. Why don't you follow up with her in a couple of days?"

Don't put the burden on your champion to find and curate what you want them to share. Make it super easy to be your champion and spread the word about your value promise using digital selling assets that require as few keystrokes and button clicks as possible.

* * *

We've covered a lot of ground here as we've talked about helping lead people from stranger all the way to champion. Will they all make the entire journey? Of course not. But the reason I drew the diagram that I shared at the beginning of this chapter is this . . .

Some people will progress through the stages of expanding their relationship with you on their own. But if you become actively involved in leading them to each next step, far more will be willing and able to make the journey.

Don't focus solely on making contact and having whatever conversations are needed in order to "close a deal." Instead . . .

1. Earn trust, rapport, and preference with people in the pre-conversation phase so that more of them will be willing to enter the conversation phase with an open mind and an interest in how you might be able to help them.

2. Take the baby steps toward the close by coming up with creative ways to enable your prospect to experience more of what it might be like to be your customer even before they commit to buy your full offering.

3. Continue to foster a collaborative partner-based relationship after they become your customer and invest the time to proactively generate repeat business, recommendations, and referrals.

Putting These Ideas into Practice

This chapter is packed with so many actionable ideas that it's almost impossible to offer a concise overview. But here's where we can start:

1. *Choose a Phase to Focus on Improving*

   Have another look at the diagram in Figure 5.1 and decide which of the three phases deserves more of your attention right now. Develop a plan to make some improvements in how you move prospects and clients from one stage to the next.

2. *Figure Out Where Your Customers Get "Stuck"*

   Determine the specific stages where your prospects or customers tend to get "stuck" or you are not seeing as a high a conversion rate as you'd like. Identify what you can do to eliminate any impediments or friction that is keeping your customers from advancing to the next stage.

3. *Capture Best Practices and Determine Your Next Steps*

   Make note of some of the best ideas shared in this chapter that you want to remember to put into practice at your earliest opportunity:

   - _____
   - _____
   - _____
   - _____
   - _____
   - _____
   - _____
   - _____

CHAPTER 6

Creating a Magnetic Personal Brand

The subject of personal branding has received a tremendous amount of attention as we continue to evolve into the world of digital buying and selling. You might be asking yourself, "What exactly is a personal brand, and why in the world would I need one?" Put simply, your personal brand is an outward representation of who you are. It's the available information that other people use to understand what you're all about. And in a digital world, your brand is out there for everyone to easily see.

The Importance of a Digital Personal Brand

Now, the truth is that you are *far* more than could ever possibly be expressed on social media, your website, or other internet destinations. But unless you operate in a world where the only impression you ever make with your customers is via live video, telephone, or face-to-face meetings, your digital brand plays a huge role in communicating the truths about you. And even if you do connect live, a lot of your prospects will "check you out" online before, during, or after you actually meet.

As far as your customers, would-be employers, or social media followers are concerned, what they see when they type your name into Google, look at your LinkedIn profile, or scroll through your Instagram posts is all the evidence they have to make judgments about who you are and what defines you. That's quite sobering to many of us who don't want to be judged solely by what people read and watch on the internet. Unfortunately, that's the way the world works today.

In a sense, you already have a digital personal brand. The question is this: Have you taken proactive control of what people *see* when they look in your direction? If not, then the impression that is formed in your customer's mind will happen somewhat by chance.

Despite the digitization of so much of modern business communication, people show a growing desire to engage with, buy from, and work for people and companies that are more "human." A digital personal brand that reveals who you are as a person gives people a chance to learn enough about you that they can come to know, like, and trust you whether they ever get a chance to meet you or not.

With the right approach, you can build a personal brand that communicates more than just your contact information and your capabilities. Your brand should give people a lens into your character, what matters to you, and what you believe in.

I like to think about it like this . . .

A strong personal brand is more than just a way for people to identify you. It's a way for people to identify *with* you!

Whether you are trying to attract employers, employees, customers, followers, or are just trying to expand your professional network, the goal is to make some sort of a connection with people through your brand. You might want your brand to help people arrive at conclusions such as:

- This person has a tremendous amount of experience in my industry.
- This person isn't just out to make a buck; they seem to really love what they do.
- Wow! They're a lot like me. Or better yet, "They really 'get' me!"
- I like this person's attitude and outlook on life.
- This person has a life outside of work. I like that!
- I can totally relate to their beliefs, their struggles, or their aspirations.

As a sales professional, or especially as a business owner, you are the face of your company. A strong personal brand enables you to stand out from the crowd. Your company may seem just like dozens of others, but there is no one else quite like *you*! Your brand can communicate what makes you unique and different from others in your space. It enables you to foster e-relationships and literally build bonds with prospective buyers and business partners asynchronously.

A personal brand is often even more effective for attracting and retaining customers than a corporate brand. This has actually been true forever— long before YouTube and social media were around. By and large, people don't trust companies. They trust the people who work *in* companies. Any trust they have in a company is based on their belief that the company is committed to hiring and employing trustworthy *people* that will treat them fairly, follow through on commitments, and do the right thing.

Personal branding is not only a way to attract prospective clients; it's becoming a major factor in how to position yourself for promotion and new opportunities within your own company or others. The traits that make you trustworthy and appealing to clients are the exact same traits that make you an attractive candidate for employment or advancement. Research has shown that over 70 percent of hiring managers use social media like Facebook and LinkedIn as part of the vetting and hiring process.[1] It gives people visibility beyond what is communicated in a résumé, an email, or a videoconference.

In this chapter, I want to share what I call the *Nine Essential Elements of a Magnetic Personal Brand*. These represent the components, if you will, of constructing a brand with *digital gravity*. A great brand pulls people in, makes them want to stay, and keeps them coming back for more.

As we go, assess yourself in these nine areas. Think about where you are strong and maybe where you could use a little improvement. But also ask yourself this question: "What am I doing—or what can I do—to let the world know where I stand in each of these areas?" When it comes to building relationships digitally, most of what people will ever know about you is what you intentionally enable them to see.

As we step into building your personal brand, it's important to note that the goal is not to try to *appear* as someone whom you think your customers would like to buy from or follow. What customers, employers, and followers respond to today is *authenticity*.

When it comes to digital relationships, we've all become a bit suspicious of the person who looks a little too perfect online. People are inundated and have become fatigued with the highly polished expert who promises hacks, shortcuts, and easy fixes to all their problems. There is something refreshing about an individual who shows up as the imperfect person they actually *are*.

That doesn't mean we want to be unprofessional, but . . .

In today's digital marketplace, being *real* is more attractive than trying to be impressive.

Many leading companies who realize the incredible leverage of creating a personal brand are empowering and even assisting their salespeople to develop their own magnetism online. Unfortunately, some organizations actually discourage the practice. To the leaders of those companies I pose the following question: If you'll pay your account executive six figures or more in base salary and commissions to be the face of your company in front of customers, why can't you trust them to upload a video to YouTube or write a post on LinkedIn? If the answer is, "They don't know how," then teach them! Or hire someone who can.

The Nine Essential Elements of a Magnetic Personal Brand

Now, let's dig into what it takes to build a brand that people not only recognize but also want to identify themselves with. I've put together a collection of nine elements that make a personal brand magnetic. They are:

1. Knowledge and Expertise
2. A Heart for Serving Others
3. A Compelling Promise
4. A Relatable Personal Story
5. The Courage to Step Out

6. Credibility and Authority

7. A Platform with Reach

8. Consistent Communication

9. Genuine Irresistibility

Do you know what I love about this list? You have the opportunity to develop or improve in each of these. None of them are beyond you! Yes, some of them will take time and effort. I certainly will never say that building a powerful personal brand is quick and easy. You'll probably spend the rest of your career developing your knowledge, expanding your credibility, and learning to communicate more consistently with your market. But regardless of where you're at right now, you can grow in each of these areas. Let's talk about how.

1. Knowledge and Expertise

Many of the most effective sales professionals and business owners are those who possess deep knowledge in their field of expertise. To lay the foundation of building an attractive brand, dedicate yourself to becoming an expert at what you do. That doesn't mean you have to become the world's most famous thought leader. But you need to know enough that other people want to listen—and will maybe even pay to listen!

Here's a solid truth worth taking hold of . . .

> **If you want to become well known, you have to know something, or know how to *do* something, that other people want to know or do!**

Yes, you need to know your business, your industry, the products you sell, and your competition. But you become much more valuable to your customer when you know *their* business, *their* industry, and *their* competition and show them how to improve in one way or another. Invest your energy learning exactly how your customers can use your products and services to increase their revenue, reduce their costs, and improve the utilization of their invested assets. Become an expert in helping your customer accomplish measurable business goals and objectives.

As a corporate sales pro, you can become an expert in the products and services you sell—your B. But, if you have technical resources and support personnel available, you're actually better off leaving that to your sales engineer or solutions architect. What you want to become an expert in is diagnosing and coming up with solutions to your customers' business problems. Learn how to uncover your customer's current state (Point A) and create a vision of a desired future state (Point C) that you can help them attain. Then bring in the technical experts to show the customer how you can help.

As you develop your expertise, showcase it online in all the ways that we spoke about in the previous chapter and many more that we'll talk about going forward. If you don't possess all the knowledge your customers need, then curate it from other sources and serve it up to them in an easy-to-digest way so they can understand it and put it to use.

If you're not the industry authority in your field yet, that's no problem. Just remember this . . .

It's not the person who knows the most, but the person who most effectively shares what they know, that becomes the expert that others turn to when they need advice.

It comes down to marketing your knowledge and expertise. If you want people to find you, you have to give them plenty of good stuff to find.

The late, great Zig Ziglar was one of the most captivating authors and speakers of the twentieth century. Anyone who ever saw him speak will say that they'll never forget it. One of the hallmarks of his speaking and writing was that he didn't conduct much of his own empirical research. What made his talks so interesting was how he synthesized information from other sources, drew logical conclusions from it, and then offered simple ways to apply it to everyday life. He always referenced the sources that he used, and that gave his work even more credibility.

You can't be a leading expert on everything all at once. Focus on a niche. Let's say you are a consultant with extensive knowledge in manufacturing. If that's you, you are among an insanely large field of competitors. But if you can focus just on the healthcare industry, you narrow things down substantially. If you wanted to specialize even further, you could focus on implantable device manufacturing in the very early phases of development, which might involve rapid prototyping and creating proofs of concept. You could potentially become a leading voice in that particular space much more readily.

If you don't have all the knowledge and experience needed to stand out in your market, then make the time to learn it. It might take years to become a leading authority, but you can learn enough to be a great resource to your prospective customers in 60 days. Get started now by simply reading several of the latest articles and watching a couple dozen recent YouTube videos that your customers would read and watch if they had time. You'll soon know enough to write some interesting introductory emails and start some engaging conversations. Then build your broader expertise over time.

2. A Heart for Serving Others

The second ingredient needed for a magnetic personal brand, which is surely as important as the first, is a heart for serving others. Knowledge alone is not nearly as compelling as knowledge in the hands of someone who has a genuine interest in helping other people. Multiple studies over the years have shown that we tend to trust others whom we believe have our best interests at heart more than qualified experts with whom we have no relationship.[2] This is true even when our only interaction with them is via the written word, images, audio, or video.

When people believe that you intend to use your knowledge for the purpose of helping others, your brand begins to take on a whole different meaning. Knowledge used for a higher purpose is exceptionally appealing because . . .

> **People may notice when they hear what you can do, but what really makes them pay attention and respond is understanding *why* you do it.**

As you seek to let others know who you are, it's important to communicate *why* you do what you do. People want to know the purpose behind your actions and intentions. When your prospective customers can see, hear, and feel that you live and breathe to help people just like them overcome the very challenges they are faced with, you become the person they will look to for guidance. If they believe you have the knowledge to help them *and* the heart to serve, you are well on your way to earning not just a customer but also a raving fan.

We all possess a certain level of discernment—to varying degrees of course—but people can usually tell when you are there to help them versus there to help yourself. They can smell it a mile away!

That's why I always like to say . . .

Just start serving your customer and helping them in every way you know how. Somehow the selling sort of takes care of itself.

One person who I think epitomizes this philosophy is Graham Cochrane (www.grahamcochrane.com), a very popular YouTube entrepreneur and influencer whose expertise is helping people create knowledge-based online businesses. Even the tagline he repeats at the beginning of every one of his videos speaks to his mission: "I'm here to help you learn how to work less and live, and give, more." Who wouldn't want some of that?

I happened to be watching one of Graham's recent videos, and when it ended, YouTube recommended the next video related to that topic. It featured a very well-spoken young woman who opened her video by saying, "I don't know about you, but I'm here to make money, build my financial future, and create long-term security for my family." Graham was focused on me. She was focused on her. Which one would you be more likely to listen to and want to learn from?

People can sense our heart by the language that we use, our interest in them, our responsiveness, our generosity to freely share what we know, and also by how we define success. Are you *driven* by your own pursuit of success? Or are you *led* by a purpose of serving others? What's the difference, you ask?

Here's the way I look at it . . .

Success is about you getting something. Purpose is about you giving something to others! Choose purpose!

People might admire (more likely envy) you for your success and trappings. But what people are drawn to is a brand with a purpose of helping others. That's who we want to follow. That's who we want to learn from. That's who we'll take a phone call from or reach out to when we're ready to further explore the possibilities.

3. A Compelling Promise

"So, what are you selling?" Have you ever been asked that? I actually love that question because it gives me the chance to answer with my favorite little comeback line: "I'm selling revenue and profit margin. Are you interested in either of those?" Remember back in Chapter 2 when we talked about the difference between Point B and Point C? To answer the question, "What are you selling?" we have to make a decision: Are we selling a solution (B), or are we selling the promise of a result (C)?

So much of modern sales and marketing revolves around *who we are and what we do.* That is packaged up into a "message" that gets broadcast via every imaginable channel. But there is a big difference between a *message* and a *promise.* A message is a statement about what *we* do and who we do it for. A promise, on the other hand, is a story that places your customer at the center of a journey. It has an origin (Point A) and destination (Point C). More importantly, it emphasizes that the customer is the one who makes the journey. The difference seems subtle, but it is actually profound! Within the promise, customers can clearly see the problem they get to solve and the result they get to achieve. You and I are just there to help guide them along the way.

Put more simply . . .

**A message is about what you do. Your promise is
about what your *customer* can do with your help.**

A promise is far more interesting and compelling, isn't it? Let's see how this might look and sound in practice.

Here's an example of a marketing message:

> *We help millennial sales professionals prepare for their financial
> future.*

This is an example of a promise:

> *You stepped into the sales profession because you have a heart for helping your customers achieve their business goals and you want to maximize your own personal income. If you're good, your sales income will provide a nice lifestyle, but it may never enable you to retire with enough years left to really enjoy what you've worked so hard for. What you do with your sales income determines how you build wealth, security, and financial independence. I will show you how!*

As you build your brand, learn to tell stories about what's possible for your customers to achieve with your help. To do this well, you have to consider the role or the persona of the person to whom you'd like to communicate your promise. Let's take another example right out of our flagship training course, *Selling to C-Level and VP-Level Executives*™.

Let's say you sell a SaaS (software as a service) solution that improves communications between your clients and their customers by enabling them to reach a customer service rep through a variety of mediums, including phone, email, text, chat, etc. That is an interesting set of capabilities, but what's the promise? We have to remember that business leaders, including those who would have to approve the purchase of such a system, don't buy products and services; they buy what I call "movements to measures." Let me explain.

Every executive or business leader is placed in charge of one or more measures or KPIs (key performance indicators) that represent the outcomes and results he or she is responsible for managing. These business measures not only reflect the effectiveness of the team they lead but are often the scorecard by which their own job performance is judged. To make our solutions relevant at the executive level, we have to learn to translate what we do into a promise of an impact on—or a *movement* in—one or more of the measures that business leader is responsible for.

Here's a great way to think about it . . .

To translate your capabilities into a compelling promise, you have to answer this question: "Which needle on which dial can be moved in what direction by how much over what period of time?"

In relation to the example earlier, rather than talking only about the capabilities of your SaaS solution, tell a story that contains a core promise something like this:

> *Based on what our clients have been able to do, your call center could reduce customer churn by up to 12 percent while increasing average recurring revenue per customer by over 21 percent in as little as 12 months.*

A photo of you in front of your yacht shows me you've made a lot of money. That can be motivating! It shows me that a lot of people must have bought something from you. That's social proof. But it doesn't necessarily persuade me that you can help me solve the problem I have *right now* nor help me achieve the goals I'm responsible for achieving going forward. As you build your brand, make sure you continue to communicate more than just what *you* do or what *you* have achieved. Make sure to help your customer understand the promise of what *they* can achieve by working with you.

4. A Relatable Personal Story

One of the most powerful aspects of your personal brand is your own personal story. Nothing engages a reader or a viewer quite like seeing how you found your way from where you once were to where you are today. This is especially useful if you are in the business of teaching other people how to do what you've already done. You can weave stories into your brand that include some of these kinds of experiences:

- Where you started out
- The challenges you were experiencing
- The negative impact these changes were having on your career and your life
- What sparked a change in your trajectory
- What you set out to do
- Some of the setbacks you experienced along the way

- How you overcame those hurdles
- What you were ultimately able to accomplish
- How your life has changed since then

All of these woven together actually makes for a beautiful story, much like the script of a Hollywood movie. Almost everybody who reads your story will be able to relate because all of us are probably in one of these stages of our own journey *right now!*

Some of the most compelling personal brands are built around taking your followers with you on your personal voyage by literally chronicling your own day-to-day adventures. People love to watch you overcome the setbacks and experience the breakthroughs. This is something that all of us can do regardless of where we are in our journey because as soon as we arrive at the destination, the whole cycle starts over again.

If you sell a product or a service—as opposed to your own advice—you can tell your own story, including details like these:

- How you found yourself in the industry that you are in now
- In what kind of a role you started out
- How you advanced to the seat you sit in today
- What you learned along the way
- The way you work with your clients today
- What personally drives you in terms of serving your clients

You can also share examples from your customers' stories as well (without sharing names):

- Challenges your clients are currently facing
- The impact on their business or on them personally
- The kinds of initiatives your clients are undertaking
- Some of the setbacks they experienced and how they overcame them
- What they were ultimately able to accomplish and how their life has changed

People love to understand the human story behind whatever you offer. It really helps illuminate your purpose, like we talked about earlier. Look at how providing just a few words about the backstory and the purpose changes this next simple example from a business description into an inspirational calling:

> *I was a stressed-out attorney working 15 hours a day. I never*
> *saw my kids. That's why I founded my* _____
> *business to help other attorneys simplify* _____ ,
> *take control of* _____ , *and get their life back!*

Now that's a story with purpose! It has an origin, a destination, and a promise! As you build, think about ways you can bring stories about your journey, or even your day-to-day life, into your brand. People who will become your followers and hopefully your customers will love the chance to get to know the *real* you.

5. The Courage to Step Out

As simple as it sounds, the thing that keeps many people from building their own personal brand is that they are afraid to step out and say, "Here I am!" I completely get it. When I started my first direct sales job in college, I would often be physically ill before making phone calls or walking into a presentation. I did it anyway! You may not feel you have everything you need to build a brand. Start anyway!

The one thing that has held me back all my life, more than anything else, is being paralyzed by constantly comparing myself to others. Log onto any social media platform and start looking at the glamorous lifestyle and daily accomplishments of the big shot content creators. It can easily seem like you'll never be as impressive as they are. But have you ever noticed that most of them are not at all in the same business that you're in? It's not even a valid comparison. Most of the rock stars on social media *are* rock stars on social media because they are in the business of teaching other people how to become rock stars on social media!

Forget all that! There will always be people ahead of you on this brand-building journey. But there are also many more who are behind or will soon come along behind. The best time to get started is right now. Here are a few things that have helped me not only in building my brand but also in just about any undertaking:

Get clarity on what you want to accomplish. Prioritize and choose one or two things you want to get done this week or even this month. Maybe it's to start a YouTube channel or set up a content development plan for the next couple of weeks. Until you define what you need to do next, you'll burn up all your energy "thinking" about what to do instead of doing it.

Find some other people to learn from. A person who's done what you want to do will be the first one to encourage you and even help you! Watch some YouTube videos or find a helpful blog post. Reach out to other content creators and ask questions. Learn from someone who's done it and ideally is *still* doing it!

Take baby steps! Get at least a rough vision of what you want to do and take one step in that direction every single day. Don't overthink your five-year strategic plan. Instead, just start taking some steps. Your vision and your plan will crystalize as you go. Seek guidance along the way, but get *moving* in a direction.

Stepping into your new role as a globally recognized thought leader can be terrifying! Fortunately, you'll never have to do that. You can't! You have to start small and work your way up. You don't have to do it all at once, but you have to do something. And the next little step is probably something quite easy to do if you just make the time and muster up the courage to do it.

Perhaps you could find an article that you think your ideal customer would benefit from reading. Break it down and turn it into the "5 Things Every _____ Needs to Know About _____." Then, post one of those five ideas on LinkedIn every morning for the next week. Make sure to give credit to the original author. Always credit your original source! Maybe tag them in your post and put a link to the original article in the comments. Take what you learn and apply it to real-world challenges your customers are faced with. You can do that!

6. Credibility and Authority

Comedian Eddie Cantor is often credited with the quip, "It takes 20 years to make an overnight success." Building a strong personal brand does not take 20 years, but it's going to take more than 20 minutes. Just imagine where you could be if you invested 20 minutes a day for the next 12 months!

Even the fastest growing influencers on social media have invested at least a year—more often two to three years—to attain a significant level of distinction. And many have invested more years than that to attract a massive following. But you can start adding followers and building your list of email subscribers the instant you start adding value to your prospective customer's day.

Establishing credibility, however, is something entirely different than just attracting a lot of social followers. Oh, a big following can help, of course. I met one gentleman who had amassed over a million followers on Twitter. That has gained him a fair amount of attention as an "influencer." It even landed him a few speaking engagements to talk about "How to get a million followers on Twitter." But the value to him day-to-day is little more than a few thousand likes on whatever dance video or cat meme he chooses to post.

Unless you're in the business of teaching people how to attract followers on social media, the kind of credibility and authority that makes you a sought-after expert in your field is not established by gaining a large social following. Having a lot of followers simply means more people get to see what you post. Credibility and authority come in other ways:

Become a Professionally Published Author

Nothing builds credibility and authority like being professionally published in newspapers, in trade magazines, and by major book publishers. Self-publishing is an option. It's a great way to get your ideas to market fast, print whatever you want, and keep more of the profit. But to build your credibility, you'll want to appear on some well-known labels with familiar logos.

You have to work your way up in publishing one step at a time. You can start by writing blog posts, articles on LinkedIn, or starting an email newsletter. Next, approach your local newspaper or business journal and write a few articles. After that, graduate to a magazine or two that your typical prospects might read. As you go, you can build a portfolio of "clippings" that you can present as you seek to publish at each next level. If you'd like a copy of a free mini-guide I created called *How to Get Professionally Published*, you can download it at: www.salesexcellence.com/handbook.

As I started building my brand, I published articles in various business journals all over the country even while I was still working in my corporate sales role. You should have seen the look on my prospective clients' faces when I handed an IT executive an article reprint that I published in the *Washington Business Journal* called "Four Reasons Why Enterprise IT Projects Fail." I wasn't just another sales rep after that! If I did it, why can't you?

Become a Podcast, Video Show, or TV Host or Guest

Getting our own show on NBC might be a stretch for most of us, but anybody can start a podcast. I'd suggest exploring being a guest on a few podcasts or live video shows first. Hosting a podcast is a great way to stay in front of a large number of prospective clients on a regular basis. But building a substantial listener base is a serious undertaking, especially with thousands of other new podcasts launching every single month!

The voice of the host is heard on every show, but the star—the one who is showcased as the expert—is the *guest*! Couple that with the fact that most podcast hosts are actively looking for guests, and it suddenly makes a lot of sense. Plus, you get in front of different audiences every single time as opposed to the same audience over and over again!

Here's a really important point to remember . . .

> **The best way to be invited to be a guest on
> podcasts, online shows, and even television is to
> become a professionally published author.**

Every host wants to feature authors because *authors* are perceived to have *authority*! Notice the same root word there? Ha!

Embrace the Art of Public Speaking

We've all probably heard that most people are more afraid of public speaking than they are of dying! I honestly can't relate at this point. I started giving presentations for a living when I was 22 years old and have spoken in front of more than 2,000 audiences since then.

People have asked me how I deal with nerves when presenting in front of thousands. Honestly, I never even notice it anymore. But when I started, I nearly passed out when I stepped up front to speak. What I can tell you is this: public speaking will build your confidence like nothing else in the world. When you can stand up in front a group of people and make sense, everything else just seems easy by comparison.

Public speaking is also a great way to enhance your résumé and build new relationships. Do you want to make a lot of great new acquaintances at the chamber of commerce? Volunteer to speak. Everyone will suddenly know you! Do you want to maximize your exposure at a trade conference? Earn your way (or pay your way) to speak at the conference. The possibilities are endless if you are willing to learn how to sell yourself as a speaker.

I started learning the trade at Toastmasters (www.toastmasters.org) and later got involved in the National Speakers Association (www.nsaspeaker .org). It truly changed my life! When you get around other speakers, you'll find they are not that different from you. They might be a little ahead on the journey, but don't let that stop you from starting now. Speak for free! Video everything you do and share those clips as you work your way up to landing paid engagements. Public speaking is one of the best ways to build your professional credibility *fast*!

7. A Platform with Reach

If you're going to develop a brand that has gravity and influence, people have to hear about you. They have to know you exist. Before the era of social media, this was an incredibly expensive and time-consuming undertaking. Now, anybody can open an account on TikTok (one of the more recent social platforms taking the world by storm), and if they happen to get lucky, go viral in a matter of hours. But posting one video that gets a million views doesn't necessarily make you influential or attract a flock of new paying customers. What you need is one or more platforms that you can use to get your story and your promise out there for people to see consistently over a significant period of time.

As you have heard and will continue to hear throughout this book, I am a true fanatic about LinkedIn for more reasons than I can even list. I can trace over eight million dollars in revenue to my company, Sales Excellence, to my personal inbound and outbound efforts on LinkedIn. You can use it in so many different ways: make a text or video post, publish an article, start a newsletter, network with other people with similar interests, or do outbound outreach for prospecting. The list goes on and on. But LinkedIn is not the only way to create or reach an audience.

You may choose YouTube or Facebook or Instagram or TikTok. The key is to pick a platform where you think your prospects hang out and start feeding into that community. Remember to lead with your heart for serving others. Don't go into it just looking for leads. That kind of an approach will probably backfire on you. People will sense it and probably be repulsed. Your service to others is what people are interested in. People who engage with you online are thinking, "What can you teach me that I don't already know?" as opposed to, "What can you sell me?"

One good way to select the right platform is to look for some other people similar to you and watch what they are already doing. If you see a couple of other people in a similar space to yours doing well on YouTube, you could deduce that there is obviously an audience for that kind of expertise on that platform. Investing your energy there could be a great choice because if those other people have all of those followers and that much engagement, an appetite obviously exists. There's a good chance that one brand will never be able to fully satiate that demand. There might be room for you, too.

Alternatively, you might observe that even though creators like you have done really well developing and serving a community on Facebook, for example, no one is really talking about your topic on TikTok yet. You could be one of the first!

If you are a local Realtor and you want to sink deep roots into a community, start writing for the local newspaper or speaking at the local chamber of commerce, Rotary Club, or other civic organization. Teach people smart ways of investing in real estate or give them tips on various forms of financing. Perhaps you could show people how to properly "stage" their home so it will sell faster and at a higher price. Start putting real estate advice in local area Facebook groups. Note: please don't just start posting your latest listings. Share insights, not ads! And always adhere to the group guidelines or you might be summarily kicked out of the group.

I want to encourage you to look beyond just social. Like we talked about in Chapter 5 on the digital selling engine, you'll want to combine a variety of different communication mechanisms, such as an email newsletter, a blog, or text updates, that enable you to reach a lot of people and make a positive contribution to their lives over time. Combine that with regular publishing, appearing as a guest on a variety of podcasts or online shows, and a bit of public speaking, and you could have a nearly limitless overall platform strategy.

8. Consistent Communication

If you want people to know you, appreciate you, and remember you, they need to hear from you *regularly*! We've all heard the old saying "out of sight, out of mind." This has never been truer than today because there are so many voices from so many sources competing for your customers' attention.

As I've already mentioned, consistency is everything, especially in social media! Well, maybe it's not *everything*. You also have to have quality content that speaks to your readers and that they can identify with. You have to provide insight and advice that is more valuable than the other posts they could take the time to read each day. But you can have all of that, and—without consistent communication and engagement—people simply will stop seeing your material and your followers may never hear from you again.

Consistent communication comes down to having a plan and some good old-fashioned discipline. Choose a frequency for publishing and *stick with it*. Maybe you could set a goal to share your story and your promise by . . .

- Posting on LinkedIn three times a week
- Posting a video on YouTube once a week
- Being a podcast guest once a month
- Publishing an article once a quarter

Start small. Develop a plan you have confidence in and can actually execute. Build over time. But whatever you do, do it very, very consistently.

9. Genuine Irresistibility

The ninth and last element of a magnetic personal brand is probably the most powerful of all. That's why I saved it for last! It actually applies to every aspect of developing your reputation and your brand, whether digital or otherwise. I call this ingredient *genuine irresistibility*. And it's not so much about doing. It's actually more about *being*.

We're going to talk about the traits of the type of person that other people want to work with and follow. These attributes reveal who you really are. They are an expression of character. These are the characteristics that everybody craves in a business partner, in a leader, and in a friend.

It is said that a tree is known by its fruit. These nine attributes, listed below, represent the fruit produced by a life well lived. This kind of fruit is irresistible. It's what everybody wants.

Whether you are a sales professional trying to attract prospective clients, an industry expert trying to build a following, or a business leader trying to foster a culture that others want to be a part of, these are the things that will make you absolutely magnetic.

Here are the nine qualities of irresistibility. Along with each of these I offer a few synonyms that help define each trait and the kinds of behavior that accompanies it. As you read through this list, think about which words best identify you and which words other people would use to describe you:

Love: appreciation, endearment, admiration

Joy: enthusiasm, positivity, optimism

Peace: composure, serenity, contentment

Patience: tolerance, even temperament, being slow to anger

Generosity: kindness, compassion, helpfulness

Integrity: goodness, honesty, consistency

Dependability: faithfulness, loyalty, trustworthiness

Humanity: gentleness, humility, respect

Self-mastery: self-control, discipline, restraint

Let's explore these one at a time:

Love

I grew up fishing the lakes and streams of southwestern Oregon alongside a brilliant and funny kid named Roger Courville. At that time, neither of us could have known that he would one day become a highly sought-after author, speaker, and a leading authority on how to run effective online meetings and conferences.

One morning a few years ago, Roger was being interviewed on the radio when the host asked a very interesting question: "How can a presenter connect with an audience that they can't see?" Roger never missed a beat. He said, "You love them!" Wow! What an incredible perspective. I truly believe this is also the ultimate strategy for how to build a brand and a tribe of people who want to follow you: You love them!

Roger says, "Your audience knows if you love them by the preparation you put into what you share, the way you tailor your presentation to the real-world situations they're faced with, and even the nature of the questions you ask. Part of it cannot be explained in observable behavior. Somehow people can just tell. When you really love them, they'll know it."

I've recently started speaking on the subject of love as it relates to sales, leadership, and organizational culture. As I begin the opening session, I have the audience break out into small groups to discuss this question: "What does love look like to your customers, to your coworkers, and to the people you oversee? How can people know that you love them?" What I hear are phrases like *showing appreciation*, *frequent communication*, *responsiveness*, and *making yourself available*.

If you love your customers, you are constantly seeking to understand what they are trying to accomplish and the challenges they face. You are always looking for solutions to their problems and ways to help them achieve their dreams. If you love your employees, you exhibit patience and humanity toward them. You hold people accountable, but you treat them with dignity and respect and as a person first.

Love is the missing ingredient in dysfunctional corporate cultures, broken families, and even in the boardroom—where we are all supposed to be on the same team. If you want to be the kind of person that other people are drawn to, be willing to express more love and appreciation for everyone around you. Love changes everything. Love never fails!

Joy

Who among us is not attracted to joy? Everybody loves to be around people who embody enthusiasm and a zest for life. Joy that abounds breeds optimism in others. When you embrace joy, people will want to hang around you on the chance that some of that exuberance might rub off on them!

One person I greatly admire for this trait is Jackie Hermes (www.jackiehermes.com), founder and CEO of Accelity. Jackie is a marketing genius and has developed a tremendous following on LinkedIn and other social platforms. What is so refreshing about her is that she tells us her own story of struggles and triumphs every single day on LinkedIn. She talks about the real fears and insecurities so many entrepreneurs face. She tells it like it is, but she shows up with a great attitude, and her enthusiasm is absolutely contagious.

If you want more joy in your life, get around people who embrace joy—even if you can only associate with them digitally.

I've found that . . .

Joy goes hand-in-hand with gratitude and hope. So, if you want to find joy, take inventory of what you have to be grateful for today and the hope you have for the future.

Can't we all be thankful for life, for our family and friends, and for the opportunity to work and serve others? There are probably dozens of other things that will reveal themselves if we quiet our mind long enough to give gratefulness a voice in our lives. If you can find any gratitude for where you are right now and any hope for what lies ahead, joy won't be far behind.

Peace

In the dog-eat-dog, hustle-centric world we live in, finding someone who operates in peace is like a breath of fresh air! If you can embrace peace, other people will want some of that peace, too. When you have peace, you'll be unflappable in the face of adversity. You'll be comfortable in your own skin. You'll find contentment for where you are even as you continuously reach higher. As you foster more peace in your life, you'll find less to be envious or jealous about in others.

Many of us simply need to make peace with our past. Some of us have done things or been through things for which we're still carrying shame, bitterness, or resentment. But as tough as it might have been—and for some of us it's been really rough—it doesn't have to continue to define who we are forever. One major step is forgiving the people who hurt us whether it was intentional or not. Holding on to bitterness is toxic. It hurts you far more than it hurts the person you hold a grudge against. Some of us need to forgive ourselves! Shame will rob you of joy and literally steal your future. Choosing forgiveness will change your life. It has certainly changed mine more than once!

Peace comes when you realize that you don't have anything to prove to anybody. You are already accepted and whole whether it feels like it or not. You are enough! And anybody or anything that tells you that you're not is lying to you and must cease to have a voice in your life. You don't have to keep striving to be complete. It's possible that you are right where you need to be for a time such as this.

Patience

One of my biggest struggles in life has been a lack of patience. I seriously doubt if I'm alone. We get so fixated on the way we think life ought to be that we forget to live life today! We sometimes have a hard time living in the present and accepting the world as it is. We want what we want, and we want it right now! The problem is that the rest of the world doesn't always align itself with our timeline. Ha!

The dictionary defines patience as, "the capacity to accept or tolerate delay, trouble, or suffering without getting angry or upset."[3] In other words, patience is about tolerance. It involves tolerating other people's opinions or behavior. This seems to be getting tougher and tougher for our society every day.

Anger, which would be the opposite of peace, has become a way of life for so many of us. We get angry with other people because of their political stance or even when they hold up traffic. Many of us need to let that go and simply accept the delays, the disagreements, and the suffering as a natural part of life. Anger and frustration only make things feel worse! Tolerance and acceptance in good times and bad is a quality that everyone is drawn to and admires.

Generosity

Earlier we talked about the importance of maintaining an attitude of service. Nothing sets you apart like being generous, kind, and compassionate to others. In the arena of brand building, being willing to help people with no expectations of a payback will make you utterly irresistible.

Of course, just because you share your advice or help your prospective customer at no charge doesn't mean they are definitely going to buy from you. We help our prospects and customers because it's the right thing to do. Buyers today naturally gravitate to people who are happy to share what they know.

Kindness is a tremendous differentiator. So, my philosophy is . . .

**Lead with generosity and let the law of
reciprocity take it from there.**

One way to keep your heart right is to remember the times when somebody helped you. Think back to the time somebody took a chance on you and the time when someone went out of their way to help you solve a problem. Never lose sight of the situations where someone else's generosity blessed you. Then, go out and pay it forward! Become the kind of person that people would describe as generous. Some will reciprocate. Some won't. It's all good!

Integrity

The word *integrity* has been so overused! What does it even mean, anyway? Integrity, or what some might simply call goodness, is the quality of being honorable, moral, ethical, and respectable. It is a commitment to what is honest and truthful regardless of the personal consequences of either loss or gain. It denotes a strong moral compass that governs everything you say and do. I also like to interpret it using the word *integrated*. To me, integrity indicates wholeness or a state of being balanced and complete.

How does this apply to selling? One person who truly exemplifies integrity in the business world is Larry Levine, author of *Selling from the Heart: How Your Authentic Self Sells You*. The cornerstone of Larry's approach is interacting with and serving your customers in the same natural, empathetic way you would treat a friend or a family member.

Integrity appears in your dealings with everyone around you: coworkers, employees, customers, etc. It is revealed in how you honor the commitments that you make.

For this reason, I like to stress this point . . .

**You can never meet expectations if they
are not properly set to begin with.**

Part of developing your integrity is carefully making promises that you know you can keep and then keeping them. Integrity is displayed when you consistently do what you say you are going to do.

Dependability

Much like integrity, dependability is being predictable in the way you respond to circumstances and the people around you. Your customers need to know that they can count on you when things don't go according to plan.

Unfortunately, this is not always evident until the customer has some sort of crisis situation, but you can demonstrate responsiveness and faithfulness even in the everyday give-and-take of commitments. Even small things like showing up right on time and getting back to people in a timely manner speaks volumes about your dependability and how much your customer can rely on you.

One of the best ways to let your customers know what they can expect from you if things go off the rails is to capture references and testimonials from the customers for whom you have gone the extra mile. One of my clients did a great job documenting this with case studies of how they came to the rescue when their customers encountered major problems. They created a series of outstanding short videos showing a dozen different examples of how their support teams went above and beyond the call of duty to keep their clients up and running and then posted them both on their website and on social media. Brilliant!

Humanity

The word *humanity* has become very popular in recent years to describe what it means to treat people with genuine caring, gentleness, and respect. Where is there room for gentleness in business, you ask? Wherever there are human beings! People want to be treated as human first. This applies to customers, employees, and coworkers. Companies are discovering that a profit-first mentality, instead of putting people first, is a recipe for losing their most talented employees, who have a multitude of choices about where and how they work.

One good example of this humanity-first mindset has been championed by Dale Dupree, a popular figure on LinkedIn and leader of *The Sales Rebellion* movement. His philosophy is that we need to stop thinking of people as "accounts" and start seeing them as human beings.

Dale contends that business is not all about profit at the expense of the very people we are supposed to be serving. We need to think about treating our customers and our employees the way they deserve to be treated. Then, profit naturally takes care of itself.

That's hardly an unheard-of idea. It's actually been around for a couple thousand years. But it certainly has been forgotten in many corporate sales environments where quotas and profitability seem to trump everything else, including relationships and even our mental and physical health. Society is beginning to realize it's time to bring more humanity into the business world.

Self-Mastery

One of the most appealing characteristics of magnetic people is their ability to maintain self-mastery. Great leaders and people that others want to follow exhibit self-control and temperance. The ability to apply self-discipline and restraint is incredibly appealing. When people see it or read about it online, they can't help but want to hear more.

I'm not talking about the guy who is hyper-disciplined to work out three hours a day, seven days a week or brags about putting in 14 hours on the phones day after day. That's not self-control and self-mastery. That's extremism! What we all want and are attracted to is a well-balanced life that blends work with family, serving others, and having a bit of fun along the way. Now that's magnetic!

Let's not forget: your brand should be a representation of who you really are. Don't try to come off as a superhuman overachiever that no one can relate to. You want to be yourself. But a life of moderation and balance tends to bring out your *best* self. Live this way and you'll inspire a lot of other people, too!

* * *

As you can see, building a magnetic personal brand is not a quick and easy two-hour project that you can complete by writing some catchy one-liners, upgrading your logo, and adding a bit of flashy graphic design to your website. Your brand is you! It is expressed by a lifetime commitment to bettering yourself every single day.

I think it's vital to remember that you're not competing with anybody else. You can never be someone else, but it's also true that no one else can ever be you. If you want to build a personal brand, put yourself out there for the world to see. I'm confident the payback will be far more rewarding than you can possibly ask or imagine.

Putting These Ideas into Practice

To put some of these ideas to practical use, I suggest taking the following steps:

1. *Assess Yourself in Each of the Nine Elements of a Magnetic Personal Brand*

   Go back to the beginning of this chapter and look at the nine elements and assess your current level of development in each. In my training session I offer a little worksheet for this purpose that is designed to illuminate where the opportunity lies to make your brand more attractive and create more gravity. You can download a printable copy of this worksheet at: www.salesexcellence.com /handbook.

2. *Pick Three Elements Where You Can Make an Impact and Do Something*

   Nine areas are a lot to tackle all at once. So maybe pick two or three to give a little attention to now. Making a commitment to expanding your knowledge and expertise is always a winner. Maybe you need

(continued)

to know more about the industry you sell to and the key business challenges faced by your ideal prospective clients. Blending that with some deeper knowledge of the capabilities of what you sell would enable you to really polish your value promise as well. Of course, committing to expanding your reach and consistently communicating with your following or your market would also make for a great high-level priority.

3. *Establish a Plan of Action and Execute*

Progress in any of these nine areas, even the area of becoming more irresistible, involves either doing more of something or doing less of something. Once you decide what you want to do to build your brand, establish some goals and turn them into tangible daily or weekly steps you can take.

Remember this . . .

> **Good intentions that don't end up in your calendar or on your task list seldom materialize into any observable progress.**

If you want to see a change in any area of life, including building your brand, you'll have to make a plan and work the plan.

CHAPTER 7

Sales Prospecting in a Digital World

S ales prospecting has been the hottest topic in this profession for as long as I've been around. Today, you can find countless books, videos, and online courses on the subject. I've even created several different courses on it myself. The fact that there is so much information on prospecting and business development suggests that there is an insatiable appetite for new ideas for how to reach people and create new sales opportunities.

Among all the other topics we've covered, I have already peppered this book with a ton of ideas for outbound prospecting. Here, I want to go deeper into the strategies and tactics while acknowledging that we will literally only scratch the surface of this vast subject. My aim here will be to talk about how to integrate digital outbound strategies with inbound demand generation to round out the overall discussion of digital selling.

Why and When to Leverage Outbound

The first question we need to answer is, "*Why* should we make outbound part of our overall selling strategy, in the first place?" As I have noted extensively throughout this book, multiple studies have shown that today's buyer shows a strong preference for asynchronous digital interactions with sellers. These statistics could be interpreted in one of two ways.

If we look at it from the perspective that sellers must blindly respond to whatever customers *say* they want, we could conclude that many companies should simply lay off their entire sales force and put all their resources into Facebook ads and a more robust transaction engine on their website. So, why don't we do that? Because many companies find that a strictly inbound approach does not produce the best results for them or for their customers.

The other way to look at these statistics is to go beyond what customers *say* they prefer in some survey and look closely at what actually converts leads into closed sales and satisfied customers. Which combination of sales motions produces the most revenue at the best margins and results in the highest rates of customer retention? I'm not saying that we should force customers to do something they are dead set against doing. But it's one thing to base our sales strategy on what survey respondents *say* when asked, "Which do you prefer?" It's quite another to actually watch what customers *do* when outbound sales motions are introduced into the buying and selling process.

One CEO of a 500-million-dollar company whom I interviewed as part of my research explained that he and his company originally launched their SaaS (software as a service) business with a straight inbound marketing model. But when they decided to test the effect of adding an outbound component to their strategy, their cost per acquisition (CPA) for new customers was cut in *half*!

He explained that it was not necessarily cold calls to complete strangers that resulted in so many more conversions. Instead, the real impact came from proactively reaching back into the early stages of the buying process to engage customers who demonstrated some early stage buying intent. This would include actions that prospects took, such as following social profiles, engaging with digital content, visiting specific web pages, downloading free digital assets, and joining email lists.

This is a powerful example of *not* just resigning ourselves to the belief that we can't or shouldn't approach our customers until they are 57 percent (or 70 percent) of the way through their buying process.

I strongly believe . . .

The best time to reach out to prospective customers is whenever they are willing to respond to the outreach!

We should note, however, that the outbound sales team in the previous example did not exclusively use the telephone as the only means of connecting with prospects. They leveraged a variety of different synchronous and asynchronous outbound motions throughout their outreach process, including comments on social media posts, DMs, and email. They also did *not* push to schedule a telephone conversation during every interaction with an early-stage prospect. They simply helped people advance through the various stages of the customer relationship journey at a pace they were willing and able to go, like we talked about in Chapter 5.

The Right Mindset for Prospecting

Before salespeople or business owners can fully embrace outbound prospecting, they have to conclude that not only is it an effective method for finding and creating sales opportunities, but that it's socially acceptable in today's business climate. There are many conflicting opinions about why, when, and how to leverage outbound. Of course, there are a thousand experts online professing that "outbound selling is dead!" But if you buy their quick and easy, foolproof system for SEO, or YouTube ads, or WhatsApp messaging, you'll multiply your revenue by 10 times in 90 days! Yeah, right.

So much of that noise becomes a justification or even an excuse for salespeople to abandon outbound prospecting altogether. And let's face it, a lot of people tend to shy away from outbound today because posting on LinkedIn or writing an article for your blog takes far less courage.

I'm here to say . . .

Inbound paves the way for more effective outbound. And outbound multiplies the results of your inbound! Do both!

As I was putting together this chapter, I had the chance to interview Mike Weinberg, the author of multiple bestselling books, including *New Sales. Simplified.* (AMACOM 2012) and well-known expert on outbound prospecting. Mike says:

> *Many salespeople feel uncomfortable about reaching out*
> *to potential clients they don't know because they feel like*
> *they are bothering them. That kind of fear-based thinking*
> *causes reactivity and even inactivity. But if you believe that*
> *what you have to offer can help them solve real business*
> *problems, you're not calling to annoy them. You're calling to*
> *rescue them!*

Think about that! Maybe we are actually doing our prospects a disservice by *not* calling them. We're robbing them of the business outcomes they could achieve with our help. If you knew their house was on fire and they were still inside, when would you stop banging on the door? Shoot, you might even knock the door down!

I've been helping salespeople maximize their prospecting results for quite a while now, and I have to say . . .

The main reason most salespeople don't see the prospecting results they really want is *not* because they don't know what to do. More often they just don't do what they know.

There are a variety of reasons why this is true. I want to take a minute to look at the seven most common reasons why we, as salespeople and business owners, struggle with prospecting and end up suffering with a weak, anemic sales pipeline that does not enable us to consistently hit our revenue goals. As you read this list, ask yourself if one or more of these could be sabotaging you right now.

1. We are not really convinced that what we have to offer actually helps the customer. We can't—in good conscience—reach out to a customer to promote a product or service that we ourselves don't believe in. If this sounds like you, go find someone at your company who can convince you of what you are worth. Better yet, ask your happy clients why they keep coming back. Let them sell you on how good you are!

2. We let fear and lack of confidence paralyze us. Not every prospect is going to respond the way you'd hope, but some will! The problem is . . .

> **If you let fear keep you from doing what you know you need to do, you don't avoid failure. You ensure it!**

Build your confidence by taking small steps forward even if you are scared to take them. Mike Weinberg says, "We have to remember, nobody has ever been injured doing this."

3. We vacillate between tools, platforms, and approaches too frequently. Often we experiment with several methods but don't commit ourselves to one long enough to get into a rhythm that starts producing consistent results. I encourage you to pick some ideas that you are learning here and run with them for the next 30 days. Don't let yourself get distracted by every new whiz-bang prospecting "secret formula" you see on a Facebook ad.

4. We haven't done enough prospecting to really get good at it. Sometimes we think, "I'm not very smooth, so I don't want to do it yet." But if you don't do it, you'll never have a chance to get good! Years ago, I heard a conference speaker say, "If you want to get good at something, you'll have to be willing to be bad at it first." So true!

5. We don't manage and prioritize our time well. It's just too easy to let customer service tasks, billing issues, and delivery problems take precedence over actual selling. We have to prioritize and establish our selling time throughout the week first and let everything else fall in around that.

6. We put forth inconsistent effort. Have you ever tried to get in shape and lose weight by exercising "once in while" and eating better "sometimes"? It doesn't work like that! Mastering any aspect of prospecting is going to take consistent effort over a period of time. Here's one truth that has helped me stay focused and consistent. . .

**Every day or week that you don't invest at least some
energy to add sales opportunities to your pipeline
means there will be a day or week at some point in
the future when you'll have nothing to close.**

That truth has helped me get moving on so many days I just didn't
want to reach out to anyone.

7. We don't have a master prospecting plan or a weekly plan of action.
If you don't know exactly what actions you need to take each week
to create a consistent flow of new prospects, you'll naturally hesitate
and procrastinate. Later in this chapter, I'm going to walk you
through how to create a 30-day plan of action for prospecting that
will help keep you on track all month long.

* * *

I have observed that most sales professionals can see marked progress in
their revenue results just by making improvements in one or more of these
seven areas, even *without* learning anything new in the way of skills training. Pick one or two of these and make a serious commitment to get better.
Set some new goals! Find someone to hold you accountable. Then, combine
this with some of the things you are going to learn in the balance of this
chapter, and you'll be unstoppable!

Tactical Versus Targeted Prospecting

Now, let's compare two different methods of outbound prospecting, which
we will refer to as *tactical prospecting* versus *targeted prospecting*. I recognize that by drawing a distinction between these two methods—tactical
and targeted—I run the risk that the targeted approach is portrayed as good
and admirable while the tactical is perceived as somehow inferior. Actually,
both alternatives have merit, but they simply have different applications.

Tactical prospecting is the method that is more traditional and where
many of us have the most experience. The more targeted method represents
the big opportunity for many salespeople and business owners. Compare
the characteristics of these two approaches in the following table. These
two approaches are different in almost every way.

Tactical Prospecting	Targeted Prospecting
Large number of prospective accounts	Small number of prospective accounts (3 to 5 to focus on at a time)
One or two contacts within each account	Many contacts within each account (5 to 10 different personas, if possible)
One medium of communication (maybe two)	Numerous and creative means of communication
Relatively generic, form-letter style approach	Personalized one-to-one approach
Somewhat infrequent and unrelated touches	Concentrated series of orchestrated touches

With the tactical approach, we make as big a prospect list as possible with the name of a key contact, such as the Director of IT, for each organization. We then decide how we want to reach out, maybe with an email blast or a telephone blitz. After that, we put together some kind of a prospecting message—which needs to apply to as many situations as possible and therefore has to be fairly generic—and send it to everyone to see who responds. Then, maybe a few weeks later, we send off another outreach to see if we can get some more responses.

From the seller's point of view, it looks like we are really working hard, sending things to or calling a large number of people. However, from each recipient's perspective, it looks as if we've sent only one isolated message with no real context or follow-through.

The more targeted method, by contrast, starts with a short list of maybe 3 to 5 accounts to target for a period of time. Rather than one contact, we would make the time to do the research and find 5 to 10 contacts of various key roles within the account (CEO, CFO, CIO, VP of sales, VP of marketing, etc.). We'd focus on the personas that we'd really like to engage with. We would then use a customized one-to-one approach that is specific to the industry, the company, and even the role of each person we're approaching. We would organize our outreach as a concentrated series of touches using a variety of different forms of communication over a period of a couple of weeks.

Because we are targeting specific individuals within certain companies, this gives us the license to really go deep in our research and preparation. It allows us to tailor our approach and what we want to communicate literally to the specific job role within the company and even to the person who currently sits in that seat.

The term *account-based marketing* (ABM) has become quite popular in the last few years. The premise of ABM is that we would market ourselves differently to each target account based on knowledge that we have about them or buying behavior we can observe. What I'm suggesting goes even deeper than that. I'm talking about role-based selling at the least and perhaps even person-based selling.

In today's world, much of the tactical type of prospecting is frequently automated, handed off to another department, or outsourced altogether. In this regard, a lot of tactical prospecting (or business development) has become more of a marketing function.

Sending out 5,000 emails that all say the same thing to 5,000 people is technically an outbound motion (we send an email to them). But sending emails or leaving voicemails in bulk functions more like an inbound technique. In essence, we put a message out there to see who reads it and calls us back.

Throughout the rest of this chapter, we will discuss both the tactical and the targeted methods, but we'll focus a bit more on the targeted approach because I believe it is quite underutilized and offers tremendous upside opportunity for many organizations. That being said, the ideal strategy would be to continue to use tactical outreach to a larger pool of prospects. And then select a subset of a small number of accounts and key stakeholders to target for a period of 30 days or so. Then we can refresh the short list of target accounts each month.

Defining the Objective of Your Approach

One of the most important aspects of any outbound strategy—whether you've created a large campaign or you're just trying to reach a particular executive with a specific company—is to define the objective of your approach. What are you trying to accomplish with your prospecting efforts?

Whether you decide to use the telephone, email, or any other form of outreach, here are some of the possible customer responses that could serve as your goal or objective. I ranked these according to what many salespeople would consider the most desirable outcomes:

1. Discover an active sales opportunity

2. Schedule a product demonstration

3. Schedule a telephone or video conversation

4. Referral to someone else internally or externally

5. Agreement to attend something like a special event, trade show, or webinar

6. Agreement to read something or watch a video and speak afterward

7. Add a subscriber to something like an email list

8. New connection via social media

Of course, some people will argue with my ranking. Rerank them however you see fit. If I were ranking these I might suggest, for example, that a scheduled video conversation might be an even *better* outcome than a product demo. Just an opportunity to talk about ourselves and demo our solutions (our B)—without a good understanding of their current situation (Point A) and their future goals and objectives (Point C)—typically yields mediocre results at best. But if a discovery conversation precedes the demo, we can earn trust and build rapport as we learn what to emphasize and focus on *during* the demonstration.

Throughout most of my career I was always taught that the main goal for every outbound motion was to "get the appointment." That *is* probably the most desirable objective for most salespeople! That's certainly what I would prefer, in most cases. Unfortunately, we typically only achieve that goal on these occasions:

- When we come across a prospect in the Top 3 percent who is buying

- When we come across a prospect in the Open 7 percent who is looking

- When we come across one of a few people in the lower 90 percent who is somehow intrigued by our approach or is just friendly enough to hear us out

But what do we do about the vast majority of the people who aren't ready for a telephone conversation yet? That's where leveraging digital assets to sell for us asynchronously becomes invaluable.

For the people in your market who don't immediately respond to your request for a live conversation, see if you can leverage one or more digital assets to do some of the selling for you. Book a meeting with everyone you can! But in the cases where potential customers are not ready, don't just relegate them to a "tickler file" and try again for a meeting in three months. There is a chance they might agree to something short of a live conversation if you ask!

Here's a suggestion to keep in mind . . .

> **If your prospects aren't ready to jump into a conversation with you, figure out a different way to help them take one more step toward you in the customer relationship journey.**

If, for example, you are doing outbound telephone calling but you are only able to connect live with a small percentage of people on your list, think about what other way you could possibly connect. If you are simply unable to secure a scheduled conversation right now, try to accomplish some other outcome from the prioritized list of objectives mentioned earlier.

A live telephone or video conversation may well be the ultimate goal, but be willing to take any forward motion *toward* that ultimate goal. If your operating paradigm is "anything short of a live conversation is a failure," you're going to have a lot of failure. I'll take a referral to someone else, attendance at some kind of event, or even just an agreement to read a one-pager or watch a video I created, if that's all I can get. Make your own list of prioritized prospecting objectives and accomplish *something* with every person you approach!

Defining the Angle of Your Approach

Another vital part of putting together an effective prospecting strategy is defining your approach *angle*. The term *angle* is often used in a derogatory sense suggesting that there must be some ulterior motive behind whatever we say or do. This might be typified by the cynical question often asked about someone of dubious character, "What's his angle?"

In this case, I'm using the word to basically ask, "What direction are you coming from?" This usage is common for editors of a newspaper or a magazine, for example, when they are considering both the topic of an article (what it's about) and the *angle* of the article (what conclusion you want your reader to draw). As you put together your approach and plan what you are going to write or say, think about the direction you are coming from.

How Will You Position Yourself?

As part of my *Power-Prospecting at the Executive Level*™ course, I identify at least five different positions that you can take when it comes to approaching an executive-level prospect. As you read these, think about which ones might play to your strengths, but also think about how they might apply to a specific account or an individual that you want to target for outreach right now. Maybe even think about the topic or the subject line for an email you could use to position yourself as one of the following:

1. Educator

- Explain how the latest technology can impact the customer's business.

- Share the latest industry trends and the impact they might have on the client's business.

- Spot opportunities and threats to the customer's business and offer a plan for how to capitalize on them or avoid them.

2. Problem Solver

- Proactively identify current-state issues or obstacles to achieving specific goals.

- Find root causes to problematic situations and craft solutions to address or eliminate them.

3. Connector

- Introduce your prospective client to other executives in their industry.

- Provide contact and access to industry thought leaders and experts.

- Bring in needed business partners to solve problems and provide capabilities beyond what you currently offer.

4. Collaborator

- Help your customer assess their current state and current levels of performance.
- Help them put together a plan to improve their performance in some way.
- Help them execute that plan and maybe even provide resources as needed.
- Help them measure the results they achieved at each stage of the process.

5. Innovator

- Bring new ideas from outside their business or totally new to the market.
- Challenge the status quo of the way they do things today.
- Help them rethink how they currently operate and then recommend process improvement and best practices.

In every situation, and especially in the targeted prospecting method, think about how you will present yourself and your company. Which of these positions might you lead with for any particular outreach? If you are able to establish yourself in the customer's mind in one or more of these ways, you're no longer just a salesperson trying to sell something. You become an advisor or a partner. Of course, in a perfect world, you would be able to pivot to any one of these positions as needed.

What Is Your Reason for Reaching Out?

A few years ago, I shot a little video with my smartphone from the front seat of my car that ended up being viewed by more people on LinkedIn than any other single piece of content I've ever created. I opened with the provocative assertion that our customers are sick and tired of the same old *lame* reasons that salespeople give for reaching out to them. I even went so far as to say using any of these should probably be against the law going forward! Here are some of the worst examples:

> *Mr. Johnson, I was just . . .*
>
> • *Checking in*
> • *Touching base*
> • *Circling back*
> • *Stopping by*

Yuck! You might as well be signaling to your customer that you are basically calling to see if they want to "buy something" today! Surely, we can do better than that.

As part of that video, I offered to share an article I wrote—which I mentioned previously—called *Seven Good Reasons for Having a Conversation with Your Customer.* Before you approach a prospective client or even try reconnecting with an existing client, think about the *specific intent* of your request for a conversation. Ask yourself, "What's in it for them?"

The following are the seven good reasons for reaching out to customers that have worked so well for me and thousands of my students. As you read them, think about exactly how you might phrase what you'd say by phone or write in an email for each of these. Maybe even write out a sentence or two that comes to mind regarding how a request for a conversation might sound coming out of your mouth.

1. Learn about their plans, goals, and initiatives going forward.
2. Teach them something relevant and useful.
3. Inform them of something they need to know.
4. Provide insight they may not already have.
5. Bring them a new "profit opportunity" (i.e., a way to help them improve their profitability).
6. Introduce them to others on your team.
7. Invite them to something special.

The practical application for each of these could take many different forms and be phrased or written in an infinite number of ways. If you want a copy of my article, which includes an extensive explanation as well as examples of exactly what you could say or write for each one, you can download it at: www.salesexcellence.com/handbook.

One common prospecting approach that is both pervasive and incredibly annoying is an email or direct message asking, "Can I have 15 minutes of your time?" Please stop doing that! Do you really want to start a relationship with your prospective client by "taking" something from them, especially their most precious resource: their time? To approach business professionals and simply ask for 15 minutes of their time for your own purposes is pretty much like walking up to someone on the street and saying, "Can I have 20 dollars?"

Instead of just asking for 15 minutes so you can "pick their brain" or "learn more about their business," sell them on what *they* will get out of investing 15 minutes with you. Perhaps you could use something like this:

> *After a brief conversation . . .*
> - *You'll know more about* _____.
> - *You'll be able to* _____.
> - *You'll have all the information you need to* _____.
> - *You'll know exactly what to do about* _____.
> - *You'll be able to decide* _____.

Here's a truth about the world we are living in . . .

These days you don't just ask for a conversation so you can sell; you have to sell your prospect on even having a conversation in the first place!

What Type of Approach Will You Use?

When using the targeted prospecting method, think about the different types of approaches you might be able to use. Here are the three most common approaches, beginning with the most effective:

Referral or Introduction

When used correctly, an introduction or referral opens more doors than any other approach. This is especially true when calling on hard-to-reach executives. Response rates and the likelihood of actually landing a meeting are far greater than with a direct (i.e., cold) approach. For this reason, as part of your preparation, invest a little time thinking about who could possibly provide an introduction or a referral so you can say to your prospect, "Bob Johnson suggested I contact you because _____."

This is always worth the time and effort. Try to garner an introduction whenever possible. Here are a few examples of the types of people who might be willing to help:

- **Internal referrals:** someone who works within the same company as your target prospect and would offer to introduce you.

- **External referrals:** a person you know outside the organization, such as another one of your clients or an industry contact who knows your prospect well enough to provide an introduction.

- **Partners and alliances:** companies with whom you already partner that could introduce you to key people. Maybe you could reciprocate with some introductions for them as well.

- **Complementary suppliers:** other companies you could form an alliance with who already have a relationship with the people you want to meet.

If you'd like more help on this topic, we offer a free tip sheet on *Networking and Referrals for Sales Prospecting* on Sales Excellence Academy. Visit www.salesexcellence.com/handbook for the link to download it.

Work Through the Executive Assistant

When trying to reach someone who has an executive assistant, there are basically two different paths you can follow. One is to work with the assistant, and the other is to try to work around them. There are merits to both, of course. But more often than not, you're going to have to interface with the assistant at some point anyway. Consequently, starting with the "work around them" approach could create tension.

I've often found that . . .

**If you want to sell past the gatekeeper,
sell *to* the gatekeeper!**

Explain to the gatekeeper that it would be valuable for their boss to invest some time speaking with you and explain all the reasons why. Help the assistant understand "what's in it" for their boss. If your story and your promise don't persuade the gatekeeper to help you find a way to get on the executive's calendar, your story or your promise might not be all that compelling to the executive either.

Direct Approach

The third way to go about reaching your prospect is the good old-fashioned direct approach. I don't usually recommend a "cold call" (a surprise telephone call out of the blue) for reaching out to executives. Although, if you want to try to work around the assistant, I've have had good success calling before 8:00 a.m., during the lunch hour, or between 5:00 and 7:00 p.m. Many times, executives will pick up their own phone when the assistant is off duty. Of course, there are a wide variety of ways to "warm up" your cold outreach, which we'll explore later in this chapter.

* * *

Any of these approaches can work. I just want to emphasize the value of the referral or introduction and the idea of working through the executive assistant. These often produce the very best results for your efforts.

A Personalized One-to-One Approach

When it comes to putting together the substance of your approach, whether you are making a phone call, sending an email, or using any other medium, always make the content of your outreach as personal as you can. Even if you are sending out a message in bulk, use customer-centric language, such as "you" and "your" instead of "we," "our," and "us." In fact, if you are writing something of any length, run a quick word count to see how many times you refer to yourself compared to how many times you refer to the customer. The more you can phrase your sentences to be about them, the more they'll feel you have their interests at heart and not just your own.

To make your outreach as compelling as possible when using the targeted prospecting method, I suggest using what I call the *Four Key Elements of a One-to-One Approach.* I recommend using these four elements in your initial outreach regardless of what medium you use. These four include:

1. A good point of reference
2. Something you've learned about them
3. How you've helped someone else like them
4. What you want them to do next

Let's look closer at each of these.

1. A Good Point of Reference

Give them your reason for reaching out:

- "Bob Johnson suggested I contact you because _____."
- "I read an article in _____ where you were quoted as saying _____."
- "Your CEO stated in your annual report that _____."
- Or even . . . "I was driving past your building last week and _____."

Make sure they know why you are contacting *them*, specifically, and not just calling anybody.

2. Something You've Learned About Them

This would include some key nuggets of information you picked up through your research and preparation that further supports why you are calling. It also helps demonstrate that you've done your homework, that you deserve their time and attention, and that what you are going to ask or say will be relevant and useful to them.

3. How You've Helped Someone Else Like Them

This is a critical element that builds your credibility and provides social proof that you know what you are doing and that you've helped other companies like theirs—ideally other people in their exact role. It shows you have experience solving the kinds of problems and achieving the types of results that might be top of mind for them, too. Use the names of companies and individuals if you have permission to do so. A little "name dropping" can be very powerful in your prospecting approach.

4. What You Want Them to Do Next

This is often referred to as a call to action (CTA). Basically, this means, if what I've already communicated seems interesting or compelling, here's what I'm asking you to do next. Traditional examples include these:

- Call me back at this number _____.
- Please reply to this email with a time for us to speak.
- Click on this link to:
  - Watch a video
  - Schedule a call with me
  - Register for our free webinar
  - Place your order

Unfortunately, in recent years, many organizations have seen a sharp drop-off in the number of people who will pick up the phone and call back. In some selling environments, it is literally unheard of anymore! Likewise, the number of people who'll even bother responding to an email continues to decline as well. In light of these changes, one effective technique when leaving a voicemail, for example, is to let the prospect know what action *you* will take next:

- I will call *you* back tomorrow at 1:45 p.m.
- I will send an email right now so you can respond whichever way you prefer.

- I will send a calendar invitation for Wednesday at 4:45 p.m. If that time doesn't work, please respond with a time that is better for you.

- I will reach out to your assistant to see about scheduling an opportunity to speak at your convenience.

* * *

Using these four elements will make every approach extremely unique, and your prospective customers will notice that! Your targeted outreach needs to sound unlike anything they are hearing from the other 26 salespeople who are approaching them on any given day.

Let's always keep in mind . . .

> **If your approach sounds so generic that it could apply to *anyone*, most people automatically assume that it *doesn't* apply to them.**

These four elements enable you to construct many types of prospecting approaches with an unlimited number of variations. You can use these four as the outline of a prospecting letter, an email, a voicemail, or even the opening talking points if your prospect picks up the phone. Now let's look at just a few examples of the kinds of media we could use for our outreach.

The Tools for Digital Prospecting

Once we've established the method we'll use, the people we'll approach, our approach angle, and the substance of our approach itself, the next question becomes, "How are we going to reach out to try to get these people's attention?" There is a wide array of options today, so let's talk a bit about the most common mediums and platforms.

As we explore digital prospecting tools, I want to encourage you with this . . .

**Don't limit your outbound efforts to only the platforms
and media you are most comfortable with. It doesn't
really matter which ones *you* like. What matters is
which ones your prospective clients respond to.**

As I talk about how these platforms can be used, some people may have a very negative reaction to one or more of these. You might think, "I would *never* send a text to someone I've never met." Or you could say, "Are you kidding me? My prospective clients would be highly offended if I approached them by sending a calendar invitation." I'll simply be making suggestions. Only you know your market well enough to decide which approaches might work best for you.

But remember this . . .

**If you reach out to your prospect believing it's not
going to work, you'll probably prove yourself right.**

I've had participants in my workshop who decided to disregard *all* my suggestions because there is one approach or platform on the list they don't agree with. Don't let that be you! What I'm presenting here is a buffet. Take what you like and leave the rest for other people with different tastes. But also keep this in mind: if you never try some of these suggestions, you may never know if they could prove effective for you.

Pick the tools and platforms you have enough confidence or interest in to at least give them a chance. I will share these in order from the most tested and proven tools to the ones that are more cutting-edge and make some sellers feel uncomfortable.

Telephone Call

The one prospecting tool that has proven to be effective for decades is the telephone. Ironically, it may well be the most terrifying for many salespeople today and is therefore totally underutilized. I observe an alarming overreliance on email as the only tool used for prospecting by many sales pros. It's not that email is not a great medium. It could be great for your environment! But as we'll talk about later in this chapter, combining various media in your approach pattern produces far better results than any one medium alone. Many of us would do well to embrace (or re-embrace) the telephone as part of our prospecting repertoire.

As I mentioned before, however, you shouldn't necessarily assume that you can go straight from total stranger to having a productive phone call just by dialing your prospective customer's number. Oh, they might answer, and sometimes you can turn that surprise call into a great conversation. But also be willing to earn a scheduled phone call by building an e-relationship first with other forms of correspondence. I find that landing an appointment for a scheduled call leads to much higher-quality conversations and better conversion rates than simply calling someone "cold."

In terms of timing, I often lean toward requesting a scheduled call at 30 or 45 minutes after the hour for three important reasons:

1. There's a better chance that they will accept the invitation or answer the call at 30 or 45 after than if you request it on the hour. They may already have a meeting booked at the top of the hour but could be finished with it by then.

2. 45 minutes after is an odd time. It makes people take notice of the request.

3. They perceive less risk in saying yes because they anticipate it being a 15-minute call.

I use the same psychology when making unscheduled, surprise calls. The latter half of the hour almost always produces better results than the first half. Here are a few other quick ideas that can help make your telephone calls more effective:

1. Check your own caller ID. Make sure your caller ID identifies you the way you want it to. People won't answer if it says something too cryptic. And if you are calling from your home office, make sure it shows either your number or your own name as opposed to your husband or wife's name. Call your provider. They can change it for you.

2. When using a mobile phone, connect over Wi-Fi if you don't have a 5G connection. The sound and the connection quality of many mobile telephone calls can be absolutely atrocious. Latency problems can cause you to constantly talk over the top of your customer. Try turning off your cellular connection and use the Wi-Fi connection through your internet service. That can make a huge difference in what your customer hears. Take the time to test what your customer is hearing before you call.

3. Get a better microphone! Most smartphones have a pretty good microphone these days. But you will be shocked at how much better an external microphone plugged into your phone will sound. There are many excellent choices for under $100 that come with the cord to plug directly into your phone. Try it! You won't believe how much better it sounds. Improving the clarity of what your customer hears on a telephone call can be a total game changer. I want every advantage I can get!

Let's keep in mind that the telephone can be used for prospecting in two ways. First, it can be the initial outreach tool (how you make the first approach) to try to earn a more extensive discussion. It can also be the tool you use to have that deeper scheduled conversation.

I want to suggest that, if you are not doing so already, you use video-conference for as many of your scheduled conversations as possible. Yes, I recognize that "video fatigue" is a real issue in today's business world. But when your customers can *see* you, it makes it far easier for them to come to know, like, and trust you. And please remember: if you want to earn trust and rapport faster, turn your camera on whether they turn theirs on or not!

Voicemail

I can remember back to the days when people actually listened to and returned calls in response to voicemails. Of course, that still happens in certain sales situations. In customer service and account management environments, where your prospects already know you, voicemail still serves an important purpose. For prospecting and reaching out to strangers, however, just leaving an isolated voicemail with no follow-up or additional outreach yields very limited results. That being said, voicemail can still be a powerful tool when it's woven into an overall approach pattern or a sequence of touches using a variety of mediums.

When you leave a voicemail, there is an expectation that the responsibility for the next action is on your prospective customer. The "ball is in their court," so to speak. I personally like to avoid that because that means I need to wait some period of time to let them get back to me. I want the freedom to place another call anytime I want, including later that same day, if I choose.

My personal habit is *not* to leave a voicemail when calling unannounced. But if I have told my prospect, "I'll reach back out to you at 3:45 Wednesday afternoon," I always leave a voicemail so they know I did what I said I was going to do. With every email, I almost always include this: "I'll also send you an email right now so you can reply in the way that is most convenient for you." The rate of response is typically three or four times greater when you leave a voicemail and send an email together than if you do either one without the other.

Email

All the latest studies show that open rates and response rates have significantly dropped off in recent years, yet email still remains one of the staples of proactive outreach. As you've heard me mention, putting the time and energy into developing an email subscriber list is truly one of the best investments you can ever make. But let's draw some distinctions between an automated email sequence sent to a subscriber list and outbound email used for prospecting.

An email subscriber list, like we talked about extensively in Chapter 4, is a phenomenal mechanism for keeping in touch with and feeding new ideas to people who have opted-in to hear from you. You can set up an automated email sequencer to regularly deliver insights and advice to either early-stage prospects who've never bought from you or current and past customers who have. If subscribers provide their contact information, such as joining a mailing list or completing a form to download a free digital asset, that provides a smooth transition from inbound to outbound where prospects, in essence, give permission for us to send them future emails.

Outbound email prospecting is something entirely different. Email prospecting more often involves acquiring a person's contact information in some way other than them giving it to you and then proactively reaching out to *make contact* for the first time.

I most often recommend sending highly targeted prospecting emails to executive-level contacts manually, one at a time, if you are willing to write something specific and personal to each individual you approach. When reaching out to a larger number of prospects with one common message, I frequently suggest using a ghost-writer (a proxy) to simply cut-and-paste a standard message manually and send it to a large number of people with minimal customization.

If you are trying to get the attention of and build a relationship with a specific person within a target account, you want your outreach to look and feel very personalized. Sending a prospecting email that is generated by an automated system frequently ends up looking like an advertisement—or even spam—and requires the recipient to "opt out" to make you go away. This doesn't make a great first impression!

Of course, there are schedulers and sequencers built into tools such as HubSpot (www.hubspot.com), Outreach (www.outreach.io), and many others that can automate a lot of the administrative work for you. They can even integrate with your CRM system to help you keep track of what you've sent to whom. Just make sure you test and ensure that some of the advantages of using these kinds of systems—such as tracking who opens your emails and whether they click on the links—don't cause your emails to be flagged by spam filters or end up in "junk" folders.

These kinds of email systems are ideal for opt-in mailing lists or large volume outbound prospecting. But for the more strategic one-to-one approach, a simple email from you to them that does not contain behavior tracking mechanisms—and looks like a simple, personal email—usually produces far better results.

There are a number of tools available today to dramatically improve your prospecting workflow and productivity. One of the best, that many of my clients are currently utilizing, is Seismic (www.seismic.com) sales enablement. It's a fantastic platform for organizing all your digital selling assets, quickly putting together exactly what you need to include in your outreach, and even sending and tracking your messages right from within the platform.

Automated "cold email" platforms designed to send out thousands or even millions of unsolicited emails can be effective for more tactical prospecting where you are canvasing a broader market to see who happens to be buying, looking, or open to a conversation right now. Woodpecker (www.woodpecker.co) is one of the best. Yes, they are legal as long as you follow the laws very carefully!

Of course, you can include links to your latest YouTube video, the newest episode of your podcast, or even a new article you posted on LinkedIn. If you design your digital assets to help readers and viewers arrive at new conclusions, they can be a fabulous addition to a written message alone. Perhaps instead of simply writing the names of a few happy clients as a means of establishing credibility, for example, you could send your prospective customer a link to a video testimonial!

Video via Email

Video is rapidly becoming the hottest thing in selling via email. Beyond just including a link to a video asset that supports what is written in the body of your email, many successful prospectors are now using video to deliver the main message of the email with very little text.

Services such as Vidyard (www.vidyard.com) and Loom (www.loom.com) enable sellers to shoot a short video using their computer camera or their smartphone and embed that right into the body of the message. Most sales professionals have at least heard of this, and many are curious, but at the time of this writing only a tiny fraction are actually using it.

This is a *huge* missed opportunity! If the goal is to help prospects come to know, like, and trust us asynchronously, why wouldn't we embrace using video as a way of life? Response rates to emails that include video are documented to be at least three times greater than response rates to emails that don't include video, and some studies show it is far higher than that.[1] Why in the world would anyone choose to approach 50 people to get three responses when they could approach 50 people and get nine responses?

Prospecting with video takes more work. Of course! But today's sellers have a choice to make. You can take the easy path by doing what you've always done and let your competitor break into your target accounts using video. Or *you* can be the one who embraces the latest technology and makes a much greater impact while your competitors sit back and watch. Which one do you want to be?

I believe that if you are doing targeted prospecting to key executives within marquis accounts, you should be shooting custom, personalized,

one- to two-minute videos as a standard part of your email campaign—
at least for one of the emails you choose to send as part of your overall
approach efforts. Why wouldn't you do that if it would increase the chances
of getting in front of a C-level executive? The pushback, of course, is that it
takes more time.

But let me ask you: if you knew that you could jump on a videoconference right now and have two minutes to share a few ideas with that exact
same executive, could you find the time to join the conference? Of course
you could! It's actually not a time problem; it's a confidence problem. We
just might not be sure it's going to work. But I think it's safe to say that if
we *don't* branch out and at least *try* using some of these newer approaches
then it darn sure isn't going to work! Don't let fear or a lack of confidence
defeat you before you ever even try. Invest the energy to do it wrong enough
times to finally get it right. What if you could master the use of video delivered via email over the next 90 days? Start this week!

LinkedIn, Twitter, and Facebook Direct Message

Direct messaging through social apps can produce some of the highest
response rates of any medium available. They have also been entirely overused and even abused in recent years. I'm sure we're all familiar with what
Mike Weinberg has labeled the "connect and pitch" prospecting tactic that
is rampant on LinkedIn now. It goes like this:

- Someone approaches you with a very unconvincing reason to
  connect, such as, "I came across your profile, and it seems we have a
  lot in common."

- You reluctantly accept because you want to increase your
  follower count.

- 18 seconds later you get a four-paragraph sales pitch and a request
  for a 15-minute appointment.

Do *not* be this person! DM is most effective after you've invested a little time to build an e-relationship and even a reputation with the person
you are reaching out to first. As I mentioned previously, I most often start
my conversation with a prospective client by leaving comments on their

LinkedIn, Twitter, or YouTube posts first. Once you've built a bit of credibility and your customer is pretty sure you're not a machine, then you might ask to connect, if it makes sense.

Once you have a connection, DMs can be a fantastic mechanism for getting people's attention. In fact, multiple studies show that it gets far higher response rates than an email even though the message is often received in the very same email inbox! DMs containing written words work just fine. But what gets an even higher rate of response is video and audio.

The LinkedIn app offers the capability to send a custom-recorded video or an audio message up to 60 seconds long to anyone you are connected with, and it's built right into the app! This is an incredible differentiator for anyone willing to use it. You decide how well you need to know the person before you reach out this way, but I have received numerous audio and video messages from connections I barely know. I have *never* refused to listen to one, and I respond to most of them, even if I'm not a prospect for them right now. Who's not going to be impressed to see someone putting forth this kind of effort to try to reach you?

I use both audio and video DM on LinkedIn for reaching out to prospective clients on a regular basis with outstanding results. It works exceptionally well with people you may have already met at some point in the past or for newer contacts as long as you approach them in a professional and respectful way. Just make sure you employ the suggestions presented earlier in this chapter for making your approach as compelling as possible. If you use video or audio to simply ask the same old question, "Can I have 15 minutes of your time?," expect to be ignored just as often as if you sent a traditional, text-based DM.

Postal and Express Mail

When I mention using written letters in my prospecting workshops, I sometimes hear, "Bill, what century are you living in? Nobody sends written letters anymore!" Exactly! That's why, when it's done well, writing letters is an outstanding mechanism for getting your prospect's attention today. This is especially powerful when prospecting at the executive level. Granted, it's technically *not* digital. But the results can be fantastic!

I've found using a FedEx or Express Mail envelope to be the most effective way to get the attention of a busy executive and his or her assistant.

Write a nice letter about why you are reaching out and ask for a scheduled videoconference. Print the letter on a nice high-quality paper. Then, toward the bottom of the page, handwrite a note in red ink pen that says something like this: "If for some reason we are not able to connect before then, I will call on _____ (specific day and time) to follow up." This technique has a very high success rate!

Handwritten Note

The idea of a handwritten note is not a new idea. Again, it's not digital, but it has been remarkably effective for decades! As people are pummeled more and more by automated email and telephone autodialers, the personal touch really stands out and can get your prospect's attention like nothing else. Even adding your handwritten signature or a short greeting on a printed mailer can be fabulous. I usually use this as one of the touches of a multipronged approach pattern, especially to key executives. It's incredible how many times prospects mention how much it impressed them.

Text Messaging

As I mentioned in an earlier chapter, a text message subscriber is about the ultimate in terms of being able to stay top of mind with existing clients or followers who highly value the insight and knowledge you provide. Likewise, one-off text messages for prospecting will almost always capture your prospect's attention. The concern that many salespeople have is that they might be stepping over a line. In recent years, I have become comfortable using text for prospecting, but only after I've reached out in some other way first.

Studies have shown an interesting generational divergence in the way people perceive the acceptability of text messaging. It seems most Baby Boomers and Generation Xers are accustomed to receiving phone calls from people they don't know but consider text messaging a much more private matter. Millennials and Gen Z, on the other hand, have far less aversion to receiving a text from a stranger but are not nearly as comfortable receiving a phone call. Interesting!

Not everyone will agree, but my feeling is that if someone's mobile number is readily available, I see no reason why calling the number should be acceptable but sending a text message to the same number is taboo. But my clients and students definitely don't see great responses to a "cold text" before sending any other correspondence. It works best when it's part of series of touches including phone, email, DM, etc.

If I'm pretty sure I have the mobile number correct—and especially if the number turns blue when I type it into my iPhone—I will usually text something like this: "John, it's Bill Stinnett. I know I am interrupting you. If you prefer to respond to the email I sent yesterday via text instead, this is my mobile number." This gets an exceptionally high rate of response!

Calendar Invitation

Another tool that is gaining more acceptance as a prospecting technique is simply sending a calendar invitation to a prospective client to request a meeting. Here again, I would not lead with this! This is something you can earn the right to send to your prospect as you invest in the relationship through multiple attempts to reach them. Your persistence demonstrates that you truly believe you have something of real value to offer.

Invitation from Your Videoconference Platform

Most videoconference platforms have the ability to invite people to a meeting. That invitation is normally sent via email, but the link can also be pasted into a text message. You can use this as an alternate to a standard calendar invitation. But this also works well for salespeople who are willing to open a conference and remain available for it during a particular period of time. You can then send a message saying, "John, I'll be in my videoconference room from 3:30 to 5:20 p.m. this afternoon. I would love to get your feedback on the materials I sent previously if your schedule permits. Join any time (include link)."

Scheduling Application

There are a number of calendar scheduling apps, such as Calendly (www.calendly.com), available today that can be used to allow people to schedule an appointment directly in your calendar. To be completely transparent, I'm not using one yet. But so many of my clients are having success with them I'll probably be jumping on the bandwagon at some point.

You can use a scheduling app in a variety of ways, such as posting your availability on your website. It can be used with inbound methods, such as posting the link on your LinkedIn profile or in the first comment on a post. Remember that the social algorithms don't like links contained within the body of a message that take users to a URL outside their platform, but a link placed in a comment works well. You can simply say "Link to my calendar in the comments below."

Online calendars can also be an effective tool for outbound prospecting. Some people embed their calendar link in the signature block of every email they send and may use a call to action such as this: "If you'd like to speak further, pick the time that works best for you from the options below."

* * *

Obviously, these are just a few of the tools available today. Who knows what will be coming out next? My hope is that you'll explore the practicality and effectiveness of every tool and platform that could possibly be used for prospecting and incorporate as many of them into your personal arsenal as possible.

The Multipronged Approach

The real magic of outbound prospecting is not any one tool or platform but weaving many of these together into an overall approach pattern designed to maximize your results. The idea of a multipronged approach is leveraging four to six or more forms of communication in an orchestrated series of touches to virtually guarantee a response from your targeted prospects. I have taught this method to over 800 sales teams over the last 20+ years with outstanding results.

If we look at using just email only, for example, we consistently see that when you orchestrate a series of multiple email touches over a period of two weeks, the response rate is three to four times greater than just sending one isolated email message alone.

However, we've seen that when you utilize a number of different forms of communication—which might include telephone (voicemail), email, DM on LinkedIn, and handwritten notes—the likelihood of being recognized and receiving a response is more than *nine times greater* than when you send one email alone.

Of course, not all of those responses result in an appointment. Some responses might include the following:

- *"I'm not the right person. You should be talking to* _____.*"* Awesome! A warm referral!
- *"Now isn't a good time. Contact me again* _____ *(timetable)."* Great! A scheduled follow-up!
- *"We are not interested."* When someone tells me this, it usually inspires me to call someone at a higher level within the company to see if everyone else actually shares his or her opinion.
- *"Take me off your contact list."* When I hear this, I never push it any further.

Some who just read that last sentence are terrified to hear that response. I don't like it either, but . . .

When you don't reach out to people because you want to avoid hearing no, you also avoid hearing yes!

The variety of media and platforms you use, the number of touches, and the frequency of outreach are totally up to you. Some will be more aggressive than others. But the multipronged approach helps get more responses more quickly! With this approach, you can determine where the opportunity lies and where it doesn't *much* faster than with just an email here and there!

I'll share two of my favorite multipronged approach patterns that are my go-to sequences. As you look at these, see if either of them seems like it might be a fit for you. Of course, you can add, subtract, or rearrange any time you want, even on a prospect-by-prospect basis if you choose. But I find that most salespeople really flourish when they adopt a pattern, use it for a while, and tweak it into just the right sequence to use repeatedly over time. You'll have to find a rhythm and a cadence that feels right for you and, just as importantly, produces consistent results! Find your sweet spot by being willing to experiment and prove to yourself what works and what doesn't.

Here is an example of an approach pattern that utilizes an existing connection via LinkedIn. The day you begin your outreach process is considered either "Day 1" or, in some systems, "Day 0." Notice that I'm leveraging a handwritten note partway through this sequence. This requires a physical address, which you may or may not have. It concludes with a video sent via the LinkedIn app. These are seldom ignored, especially after all the other work you've put into trying to initiate a conversation.

Day 1: LinkedIn text DM

Day 3: Email #1

Day 6: Telephone (voicemail) #1

Day 6: Email #2

Day 8: Handwritten note

Day 11: Telephone (voicemail) #2

Day 13: Text message

Day 14: LinkedIn video DM

Here is a different pattern option that works quite effectively for approaching an executive who has an assistant. Here I'm leveraging the FedEx letter, which requires a physical address, as well as a meeting invitation.

Day 1: FedEx letter

Day 4: Telephone (voicemail) #1

Day 4: Email #1 to the executive

Day 5: Telephone (voicemail) #2

Day 5: Meeting invitation

Day 9: Email to the assistant

Day 13: Telephone call to the assistant

Day 14: Email #2 to the executive

It is very rare to work completely through either of these patterns and not get a response. I won't say I have a 100 percent response rate, but it's very high. I don't always get a meeting, but I get a response! Some approaches advance to conversations. Some don't. It's all good!

Please note that these are simply two examples of an unlimited number of approach patterns that you could employ. The key is to come up with a pattern in which you have confidence. Use it for a few weeks, and then tweak it and perfect it as you go. But as I mentioned earlier, you have to commit to something and prove it out. Don't just try it one-and-a-half times before you deem that "it doesn't work."

30-Day Prospecting Plan

To help salespeople develop their own road map of how to apply what they learn in our prospecting workshops, I created a tool that I call a 30-Day Prospecting Plan that really breaks it all down into seven easy steps.

Please note: the outline of this plan will serve the purpose of the "Putting These Ideas into Practice" section found at the end of every other chapter in this book.

This is a great tool to help you put together a good track to run on for the next 30 days. At the end of the month, assess how you did. You may want to tweak your activity goals, select a few new target accounts, change up your multipronged approach pattern, or allocate your time differently.

This kind of plan has proven to be absolutely invaluable for literally thousands of salespeople who have put it to use after coming through one of our prospecting workshops. If you want a copy of the fillable PDF tool, you can download it at: www.salesexcellence.com/handbook.

This is a strategic plan that will help you focus your energy on your targeted prospecting efforts within a few select accounts. Let's walk through these seven steps together:

1. Set some business development goals! Determine exactly what prospecting results you want to accomplish and why. Determine the number of opportunities you want to add to your pipeline this month. Think about how many client visits you'd like to hold each week, the numbers of approaches you want to make each day, or the

number of new deals you want to add to your pipeline by the end of the month. Your goals are both your motivation to do the work and your yardstick to see if you are making progress.

2. Decide which companies, divisions, or business units you will target that would be ideal additions to your client list. This speaks to creating your short list of target accounts. Pick companies that are in the right industry and location, are the right size, and, most importantly, that you would be really excited and proud to do business with.

3. Decide which people you will target within each company. Which ones would most likely play a role in a buying decision? Rather than starting with just one name, identify multiple contacts by taking the time to research and select a number of different people in each organization you target. This increases your chances of success and reduces the time it will take to get a response.

4. Decide which mediums of communication (letter, phone, voicemail, email, text, LinkedIn, WhatsApp, etc.) will be part of your approach pattern. Develop a multipronged approach pattern that you are excited about and start employing consistently. You'll tweak it as you go. But make sure to test your pattern enough to really determine what's working and what's not before you totally change it up.

5. Decide which planning and tracking tools or templates you will employ to organize and track your efforts and results. Think about where you will keep track of who you reached out to, on which date, and in which way. Use your CRM system if you can. Otherwise, a spreadsheet or even a trusty old notebook will work.

6. Decide how much time you will invest in business development on a daily or weekly basis. Manage your time carefully! This might be the hardest step of this plan. There are just so many things that can cause distraction. I recommend blocking the hours you will dedicate to prospecting for the entire week before the week even starts. Guard that prospecting time ferociously!

7. Execute relentlessly for the next 30 days. Don't let anything knock you off track! Then, reassess and plan for next month. This final

piece boils down to discipline and focus. That's the reason it's so important to think about "why" in Step 1. Without some burning desire to accomplish something, it's too easy to lose momentum and give up. Know your *why* and keep it in front of you! If you need to, find someone to help you stay accountable to yourself!

* * *

An end-to-end discussion of sales prospecting, and especially all the technology enablement and automation tools available today, would fill 100 books or more. In fact, it already has! And long before this book ever makes it into your hands there will be new technologies and tactics that don't even exist at the time of this writing. If outbound prospecting is something you are responsible for or interested in, come join the conversation about prospecting and digital selling on LinkedIn. Connect with me at: www.linkedin.com/in/billstinnett. I can't wait to share the latest ideas that have been working for me and hear what's been working for you!

CHAPTER 8

Managing and Closing Deals Digitally

The potential for using digital assets to find and create sales opportunities is truly limitless whether we adhere to strictly inbound strategies, choose to leverage outbound, or use a combination of the two. In this chapter we are going to look beyond just opportunity creation and explore how we can employ digital assets throughout our customer's buying process to manage and close the deals we've created.

Some sales environments lend themselves well to fully automating interactions with prospective customers. In endeavors such as online retail, self-service websites, or even the sale of many SaaS solutions, business can be conducted with no person-to-person communication between the buyer and the seller. In those situations, *all* of our selling has to be done via sales copy, graphics, audio, or video. As we move through this chapter, we will explore how we can use various kinds of digital selling assets in that scenario as well as in more complex sales environments where some amount of person-to-person selling is required.

In Chapter 1 we talked about being able to interact personally with buyers during only 5 or 6 percent of their overall buying process in some cases. As our customers move upward through that pyramid of awareness we talked about in Chapter 2, and even once they start actively looking at and exploring possible suppliers, our access to the various influencers and approvers within our customer's organization can be quite limited. For that reason, I recommend creating a variety of digital selling assets that are designed to help customers advance through their buying process even when we are not around. A tremendous amount of selling can be done asynchronously in between conversations with our customer.

Your Customer's Buying Process

Early on in my sales career, I was fortunate to have the opportunity to attend a lot of really great sales training courses. They covered topics like prospecting tactics, closing techniques, and negotiation skills, but what really fascinated me was managing the overall sales process. I was committed to mastering what many of those authors and speakers purported to be the "step-by-step process" to close every sale. I became obsessed with it.

As I read every book on sales I could find and listened to hundreds of cassette tapes (i.e., recorded teachings), I organized my own six-stage process for selling the kinds of complex technology solutions my company offered. Most salespeople today have seen something like this. Figure 8.1 shows how a sales process can be organized into five, seven, or any number of stages.

The sample sales process in Figure 8.1 is made up of these six stages:

1. Identify
2. Qualify
3. Validate
4. Propose
5. Close
6. Deliver

You'll be delighted to know that I'm *not* going to ask you to adopt and use my process. Quite the contrary! I want you to develop your own process for selling what you sell to the kind of clients you serve. One thing I learned along the way is that the sales process can vary greatly based on the nature of products and services you offer, the kinds of companies you serve, and the price point of your solutions.

Figure 8.1   Defining Your Sales Process

Identify	Qualify	Validate	Propose	Close	Deliver	
Discover account and potential opportunity	Understand business goals, disparities, and action drivers	Obtain executive sponsorship	Deliver solution overview and value proposition	Provide references	Smooth handoff to client services	
Conduct account research and analysis	Understand buying process, influencers, and approvers	Conduct needs analysis	Size and scope implementation	Present final proposal to all influencers and approvers	Ensure all promises kept and expectations met	
Identify players		Validate desired business results	Introduce pricing	Submit final contract for all needed approvals	Monitor all deliverables (as appropriate)	Things We Do
Understand current state "A" and desired future state "C."	Propose process of mutual discovery	Confirm project support priority, timing, and budget	Demonstrate and prove solution for approvals	Negotiate contract terms . . . if necessary	Monitor collections (as appropriate)	

If you sell for a corporation, there is a good chance that you already have a defined process and a CRM system to help you track opportunities through it. It helps! Utilizing a sales process has helped me, and I've seen it help thousands of salespeople I've trained and coached over the years. Having a documented process to follow and perfect over time is a vital part of consistency in pipeline management and forecasting. A good process gives us guidance on what to do next, helps us not forget important steps, and becomes a framework that allows the entire organization to work together using a common language.

Here's the problem. I spent the first several years in this profession so focused on the steps I was taking and what I was trying to accomplish that I was literally oblivious to what was actually going on in my customer's buying process. This is rampant within sales organizations to this day. We tend to get so wrapped around the axle of our sales process that we never even think about all the little decisions and the steps that our customer has to work through in order to buy.

Somewhere along the line I finally learned . . .

> **The whole reason that we have a sales process
> is to help our customers work through the steps
> and stages of their buying process.**

Success in the selling profession is not based on what *we* do. We book revenue, retire quota, and get paid based on what *our clients* do. When a customer decides to take action and buy something, *then* we make some money. Therefore, the steps we take to try to sell something really should be based on helping our customers take the steps they need to take in order to buy something. Our job as a sales professional is to help facilitate our customer's buying process. To depict this truth, I created the diagram in Figure 8.2.

The chevrons and the boxes across the top define the "things we do" as part of our sales process, while the chevrons and boxes across the bottom show the "things customers do" as part of their buying process. Here are the six stages of a typical complex buying process, as I have defined them:

1. Recognize

2. Explore

3. Evaluate

4. Select & request

5. Approve & commit

6. Implement

While many of us have already learned this, either intuitively or through previous training, I've found that for a lot of salespeople, looking at this diagram produces a significant aha moment.

This model represents a very generic example of what a buying process might entail. Here's my question: "Can you sit down and write out the steps and stages *your* typical customer has to work through in order to buy?" It's one thing to know this *in theory*. It's another to consistently put this into practice and literally help your customer work through the steps and stages they have to work through.

I want to challenge you to carefully define a typical buying process for the kinds of products and services you sell. You might need to lay out more than one if you have a variety of offerings, especially if you sell some inexpensive products, some big-ticket products, subscriptions, professional services, etc. The key is to put yourself in your customer's shoes and see the buying process from their point of view so you can help them work through it a step at a time.

Figure 8.2   Understanding Your Customer's Buying Process

Identify	Qualify	Validate	Propose	Close	Deliver	
Discover account and potential opportunity Conduct account research and analysis Identify players Understand current state "A" and desired future state "C"	Understand business goals, disparities, and action drivers Understand buying process, influencers, and approvers Propose process of mutual discovery	Obtain executive sponsorship Conduct needs analysis Validate desired business results Confirm project support priority, timing, and budget	Deliver solution overview and value proposition Size and scope implementation Introduce pricing Demonstrate and prove solution for approvals	Provide references Present final proposal to all influencers and approvers Submit final contract for all needed approvals Negotiate contract terms . . . if necessary	Smooth handoff to client services Ensure all promises kept and expectations met Monitor all deliverables (as appropriate) Monitor collections (as appropriate)	Things We Do
Recognize or acknowledge disparity Conduct needs analysis Identify linkage to business goals and objectives Explore action drivers and prioritize	Explore existing solutions Contact possible new partners or suppliers Identify buying process, influencers, approvers Establish process and evaluation criteria	Establish executive ownership (oversight) Validate desired business results Evaluate and vet potential suppliers Confirm project priority, timing, and budget	Approve solution overview and value proposition Plan implementation Quantify ROI and justify investment Select vendor of choice and submit requisition	Check references Finance obtains or releases funding Legal approves contract Final approver signs off Contract signer signs contract and/or issues purchase order	Management provides support and resources for project Execute implementation plan on time and budget Monitor all deliverables from vendor Pay bills on time	Things Customers Do
Recognize	Explore	Evaluate	Select & Request	Approve & Commit	Implement	

The Missing Stage of the Buying Cycle

What these various steps and stages represent is a process your customer works through to get from Point A—where they *recognize* some kind of a problem or need—to Point B, where they *commit* to buy something, then through the *implementation* stage as they work toward Point C, where they hopefully obtain their desired result.

One interesting observation I like to share is . . .

> **The instant your customer arrives at Point C, it becomes the new Point A. What was once the desired future state is now the new current state, and the whole process starts all over again.**

What I want to spend some time on now is understanding *how* it starts over. What we'd like, of course, is that once we help our customer derive some kind of desirable outcome, they would want to delve into the next project with us. If we help them achieve their goals and objectives, why wouldn't they want to work with us again? Great question! What we have to think about is: "Once we get to Point C, what happens after that?"

Notice that the buying process, as I have laid it out here, is a series of steps and stages our customer works through to get from one place to another. I've seen hundreds of diagrams depicting the sales process like this over the years, and they all share this same characteristic: a process has a beginning and an end. But to turn this six-stage buying process into a repetitious *cycle*, where the customer buys from us again and again, we have to add a seventh stage. I call this the missing stage "Assess & Measure" as shown in the customer buying cycle in Figure 8.3.

Figure 8.3 The Missing Stage of the Buying Cycle

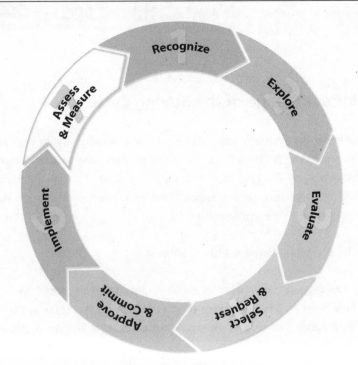

Thinking back to my enterprise software sales days, I recognized the incredible value our clients saw in having our help to establish project milestones and key performance indicators—before a project ever started—that they could use to track their return on investment over time. We helped them assess their current performance using a variety of business measures to create a benchmark at Point A. This actually functioned as a terrific justification for why they should buy from us and undertake the project in the first place.

Once we had a scorecard or a yardstick of sorts, we could use that to assess and measure their performance again at specific intervals as they progressed toward their desired future Point C. This practice not only helped our customers stay focused on ensuring they got the payback they had envisioned when they made their investment, but it quite often became the way they would recognize a *new* dissatisfaction at the new Point A, which led to the *next* project with us!

I've lived by this philosophy since the day I opened the doors at Sales Excellence. From the beginning we developed an entire framework that helps our clients establish benchmarks and track their progress on a variety of vital performance measures. I want to encourage you to do the same thing!

If you want to drive customer satisfaction and repeat business at the same time, learn how to help your customers assess and measure themselves against their own past performance and, even better, against similar companies in their space. I have found time and again that helping customers gauge their performance naturally reveals opportunities for improvement. Assessment and measurement drive recognition of the next business problem to overcome and the next goal to pursue!

This means that . . .

Helping your customers assess and measure their performance isn't always the seventh stage in their buying cycle. In many cases, it can actually be the *first* stage!

I encourage you to invest some time and energy to come up with one or more creative ways to help your prospects assess themselves and their business even before they ever become your customer. You can do it for free, you can make it a mini-offer for which you charge a little, or you can make it into a robust service offering and charge a lot. Thousands of companies are "in the business" of helping clients assess and measure their performance in variety of ways. It can be an entire business model in some industries.

I think almost any company could potentially offer some form of assessment and measurement that would help drive the recognition of customer needs and gaps between where they are and where they'd like to be. This could be as elaborate as a three-month paid needs assessment project or something as simple as a slogan: "Got milk?"

Facilitating the Buying Cycle Asynchronously

If we had unlimited access to the key decision makers and influencers within our customer's organization throughout their buying process, we could help facilitate every step firsthand. We could offer information and guidance in each phase of the process via telephone, videoconference, or face-to-face meetings. However, because our "face time" is more limited these days, we should think about how we can take much of what we might share in person and capture that in one or more digital formats that we can use to advance the buying process even when we can't arrange a real-time conversation.

As I mentioned in Chapter 3, some of these assets can be broadly distributed for public consumption. Others should probably be reserved to share only with qualified prospects. And only at the specific time that they need to use them as part of their evaluation, selection, approval, and purchasing processes. Certain proprietary information and videos need to be shared only privately to minimize exposure to our competitors or prospective clients who simply aren't ready to understand and assimilate them yet.

To help with planning out what kinds of digital assets and selling tools might be most important to develop for your purposes, I offer the following four steps:

1. Map out a typical buying process for the types of customers you work with. I just issued this challenge a few pages ago. As I

mentioned, you might need two or more of these depending on how many different kinds of products and services you offer. Don't overcomplicate it. Just pick one for now and define the steps and stages your typical customer has to work through, so you can think about what kind of digital assets might be helpful to them at each stage. In my workshops, I provide a really handy worksheet to use for this called *Understanding Your Customer's Buying Cycle*. You can download a copy at: www.salesexcellence.com/handbook.

2. Determine which buying roles might be involved at each stage. Think about the actual personas who will play a part in each of the major steps. For example, you might have a technical approver involved at some point in the buying process. Think about what he or she might want to hear or understand if you had unlimited opportunity to meet with them. If you know that you'll have a financial approver involved in some aspect of the purchase, give some thought to what that person might need from you to streamline and even speed up the funding and purchasing process.

3. Think about what guidance and information you and your company could provide at each step. According to the Gartner study I referenced in Chapter 1, the average customer spends 45 percent of their time in a complex buying process doing online and offline research. Wow! They spend another 22 percent of their time meeting with other members of the buying group. We should think about— and even talk to some of our friendly customers to learn about—the nature of that research and what is usually discussed in those meetings.

    What sources are they going to for information? What kind of information is the most helpful to them as part of their research? What are the topics of some of those internal conversations, and what could we provide in terms of insight and knowledge that would make those meetings more productive? Once we know that, we can create assets and resources to serve that exact purpose.

4. Decide what format or platform to use to share your guidance and information. You can capture your expertise and deliver your knowledge asynchronously in many different formats. You might even want to offer something like *Five Tips to Eliminating Delays*

in *Purchasing* as both a PDF checklist *and* a video for some who prefer to read and others who might rather watch or listen. Some of the tools I'll mention later lend themselves nicely to one format or another. I've discovered clients appreciate seeing a variety of formats for these kinds of assets. If, on the other hand, every single digital asset you share is a PDF document, all those documents can become a little monotonous and uninteresting after a while.

When to Insist on a Synchronous Conversation

Some of what we need to share with our customer throughout their buying process can be packaged quite effectively as asynchronous communication. Likewise, some of the questions we need to ask can be handled quite easily via email. But there are certain points in a selling/buying process—especially where larger transactions and more complicated solutions are involved—where a real-time conversation is required. I'll go so far as to say that trying to facilitate some of these steps asynchronously can be a recipe for disaster.

As you map out your typical sales process, you may identify several steps that are best handled live. There are three major reasons why this might be best:

1. We might need them to confirm that we understand *them* correctly.

2. We need customer feedback, confirmation, or agreement with what we recommend or propose.

3. We need to *close* on the next step in the buying process, such as one of the following:

   ○ Introduce us to some other key person in the organization

   ○ Approve our recommendations

   ○ Agree to take the next step in their process

   ○ Sign the contract

Here's what we all need to remember . . .

The one huge drawback to asynchronous selling is that you forfeit the opportunity to ask for a commitment and wait for them to agree in real time. You lose the ability to truly *close*!

If you're like me, you read this and think, "Well, then I don't want anything to do with asynchronous selling. I don't *ever* want to lose the ability to close!" But we have to remember that for every critical step that requires us to obtain a commitment from the buyer, there are six or seven other steps the customer needs to take that can be supported quite beautifully using digital selling assets.

Once again, I'll say that some sales environments demand more real-time interaction than others. But for more complex selling/buying processes, here are at least four major steps where a real-time conversation is absolutely crucial. Notice that in each of these cases, we need customer confirmation and feedback to deem this step a success and advance to the next step in the buying process.

Discovery and Needs Assessment

In recent years, I've seen some of my clients having great success with online surveys and questionnaires to help assess a customer's needs prior to a live discovery call or a demonstration. These can be akin to the type of questionnaire that you might fill out at a doctor's office prior to being examined, just to document and expedite the transfer of information.

But if you sell big-ticket solutions in a competitive market, you're going to want to insist on a live discovery call. There's just too much at stake to step into a product demonstration—or especially into a solution presentation or a proposal—without being able to ask some questions to make sure you are presenting or proposing the right thing. And, just as importantly, the discovery call is one of the best opportunities to earn trust, build rapport, and justify meeting key decision-makers. If you're selling complex solutions, a live discovery call (maybe multiple calls with multiple stakeholders) is an absolute must!

Custom Solution Demonstration

Some products lend themselves nicely to being demonstrated via prerecorded video. If it's a product that has a fixed set of features and you can showcase enough of them to make a sale on video, that's great. But if what you offer has extensive capabilities or can be configured and implemented in a variety of ways, you'll want to do a custom demo live, and you'll need to have held a good discovery call ahead of time so you know what to show.

You could do a prerecorded, screen-movie demo based on your discovery, but you'd ideally like to be able to get real-time feedback from the client and help them work through any confusion that may come up. Many of the questions that are asked during product demonstrations provide great opportunities to draw differentiation between you and competitors or to really help solidify your customer's choice decision.

I also always use the custom demo as the justification for meeting with more of the stakeholders involved in the decision process. My thinking is this: "If we're going to put in the time and energy to provide a custom demonstration, then you (Mr. Client) need to bring all the right people who need to see it into the room or on the videoconference." At the end of the meeting, I want to be able to close by asking, "Are there any other outstanding questions, or are you ready to make the commitment to move forward with the purchase?"

Presenting Proposals and Pricing

As I already mentioned, there are times when real-time feedback is just flat-out required. It's especially important when you present pricing. There are several reasons for this. First, you need to always make sure the customer understands exactly what they are getting for the money. If you just email a proposal, there is a good chance they won't even take the time to read it properly. Oftentimes, they'll just flip to the last page where the pricing is listed and give themselves sticker shock. And even if they do read it all, the probability of misunderstanding at least part of it is nearly 100 percent.

If the size and scope of what you are proposing is significant enough to warrant it, go see your customer in person or at least get them on videoconference to walk them through the entire proposal. Make sure they understand exactly what they will get and quantify the value and the pay-back *before* you get to the price. Then you can ask a closing question like this: "Based on everything we've discussed, are you ready to move forward with the project?"

The biggest mistake I see salespeople making today is sending propos-als and pricing via email and waiting to see if the customer calls them back. Stop doing that! That is *not* digital selling. That's just throwing a price in their direction and expecting them to close themselves, which very seldom happens. Get ahold of them live, explain everything, and ask for their feedback. Then you can address any questions they may have, clear up misunderstandings, and help them work through any concerns or heart attacks that may arise related to pricing.

Negotiation and Closing

It is possible to go back and forth with your customer to negotiate pricing or other terms and conditions via email, but it's not ideal. As part of our *Clos-ing and Negotiating for Maximum Profitability*™ workshop, we stress the importance of asking questions to determine the nature of any request for concession that a customer might make. Is it a simple misunderstanding? Is there some condition of the sale we need to work around? Or are they just "fishing for profit?"

It's impossible to really get to that level of discernment outside of a syn-chronous conversation. To drill to the motive of their request, understand their perception of a mutually beneficial resolution, and gauge their recep-tivity to your recommended trade-off, you have to be talking to them live.

Keep in mind that your customers are attending seminars on negotiating with suppliers (like you) and are being taught a myriad of techniques and tactics to throw you off balance, including trying to avoid a live conver-sation. Don't fall for it! If they want to do business with you, assure them that you'll do the best you can for them but insist on *talking* to them to do it. My habit is to propose something like, "I'm confident we can come up with an agreement you'll be happy with. I'm available to work it out *on vid-eoconference* Thursday at 2:00 p.m. or Friday at 10:00 a.m. Which is best for you?"

Using Digital Assets in Every Stage of the Buying Cycle

I strongly believe there are digital assets we could create that would enable us to better facilitate the buying process at nearly every step through all seven stages. Now, let's take a closer look at each of these seven stages of your customers' buying cycle as well as the kinds of conclusions your customer will need to draw and the decisions they'll have to make in each of them.

I will offer just a few examples of sales assets that could be used in each stage. In some cases, I will recommend a format. In others I might just throw out a title that could take the form of a free guide, a video, a checklist, or whatever you think would work best.

As you read these, I want to encourage you to grab a piece of paper and a pen and write down whatever comes to your mind about the kinds of tools or assets that you could employ in each of these stages. Even go so far as to imagine what format might be best and write down some possible titles or descriptions that are appropriate for your business.

If you work for a larger company, you can probably find a ton of sales collateral and tools that already exist, if you ask around a little bit. If you don't have anything and you just aren't ready to build a set of digital assets of your own, search the web to see who has already published something like what you have in mind. You could even *use* some of the sample assets you find until you have time to create your own!

I'm convinced that if you're willing to make even one of these, you could immediately start using it to close more business. That would be a great success! And if you can create *one*, you can create more!

1. Recognize

In this stage, a customer recognizes some dissatisfaction with their current state (A). It might be that they've fallen short of some stated goal or objective. They could be missing deadlines, failing to meet customer expectations, or experiencing declining profitability. Along with this recognition, they would also likely conclude that the consequences of doing nothing are just too great and there is an urgency to take some action now.

Here are some examples of digital assets that we might be able to provide that would help them in this stage of their process:

White paper: *How Top* _____ *Companies Spot Gaps in Critical Success Metrics*

Free guide: *5 Root Causes That Lead to* _____ *Failure. Here's How You Can Correct Them!*

Article: *7 Key Metrics That Every Executive in the* _____ *Industry Must Monitor Carefully*

LinkedIn post: *3 Ways You'll Know When It's Time to Upgrade Your* _____ *System*

Notice that all of these examples relate to some form of assessment that will drive recognition of a dissatisfaction with their current state (Point A). That's why I stressed earlier that the assess and measure stage, which I usually list as Stage 7, is often the *first stage* when it comes to helping customers recognize problems and opportunities for improvement.

Assuming your customer has already recognized a need, pain, or problem with the current state (A), they might be able to benefit from some insights, such as the following:

Video: *5 Key Steps to Conducting Your Own* _____ *Needs Analysis*

White paper: *4 Ways to Quantify the Consequences of* _____ *(common problem you solve)*

Free guide: *A Step-by-Step Guide for* _____ *Root-Cause Analysis*

Checklist: *7 Vital Steps to Conducting Your Own Feasibility Study*

Article: *So, You Think You Need to Upgrade Your* _____ *System. Now What?*

2. Explore

Now that your customer has determined they have a problem and they really need to do something about it soon, they naturally start looking for solutions and the people who can help them solve it. They move into the explore stage. Keep in mind that there is often far more to solving business problems than just buying a product or a service. They may not even have determined they need to make a purchase yet.

If your customer does decide they need to buy something, they often look to their existing partners and suppliers first to see what they could possibly provide. They might start to think about gaining internal support, consensus, and maybe even securing funding to help solve this burning problem. Think about how assets like these could assist in your customer's decision-making process:

Video: *Top 3 Ways to Eliminate the Problem of* _____

LinkedIn post: *6 Ways to Determine If It's Time to Switch* _____ *Providers*

White paper: *The Pros and Cons of Outsourcing* _____ *Versus Doing It In-House*

LinkedIn article: *4 Critical Capabilities to Look for in a* _____ *Solution*

Blog post: *5 Steps to Gaining Consensus and Support for Your* _____ *Project*

Free guide: *A Step-by-Step Guide to Securing Funding for* _____

3. Evaluate

In the evaluate stage of their process, your customers will not only start looking at possible providers but also start thinking about:

- Establishing responsibility and project oversight
- Validating the business impact of a purchase and the associated project
- Confirming that they have support from all the relevant stakeholders
- Determining if this investment will produce an ROI attractive enough to get funded

A few digital assets that might help do some of the selling in this stage could include the following:

Article: *4 Reasons Why* _____ *Projects Fail.* This is similar to the article I published in the *Washington Business Journal* (which I mentioned in Chapter 6) that was written to expose some of the pitfalls for executives to avoid as they worked through their selection and implementation processes. One of them was failure to establish responsibility and oversight. Another was poorly defined project goals and objectives. A tool like this can be a terrific way to advise your client on how to properly evaluate and assess the viability of an upcoming investment and mitigate the risk of failure at the same time.

Checklist: *7 Pro Tips for Evaluating Possible* _____
Providers. Write this in the voice of your customer. Perhaps even feature seven of your best, most well-known customers who provide one pro tip each. This can be an incredibly powerful selling tool. Make one of these for your company ASAP!

Blog post: *How to Secure Executive-Level Support for Your* _____ *Project Before You Ever Start.* Wouldn't your prospective client love to know whether they are able to garner the support they need for a new project before they spend a ton of time working through their choice decision (as discussed in Chapter 3)?

Spreadsheet template: *Business Case Calculator to Justify Your Investment in* _____. Most companies who are considering spending a lot of money with you will have to produce a business case to justify the investment and obtain funding. One of the best things you can do is provide some guidelines or maybe even a template to help them with that process. This can save your customer a great deal of time. They will love you for it!

4. Select and Request

During this stage, your customer will be working through the steps of selection and requisition. It may be obvious what kind of information they are requesting from would-be providers, such as presentations, proposals, and responses to RFPs (requests for proposal). But we also need to give some serious thought to the steps that the customer has to take within their internal buying process. Some of these steps might include the following:

- Evaluating proposals or RFP responses
- Planning an implementation
- Creating and submitting a business case or cost justification
- Submitting the purchase requisition and all associated paperwork

Here are some ideas for digital assets that might be useful to your customer:

Blog post: *4 Things to Look for in Your* _____ *Partner That Will Never Show Up in an RFP Response*

Spreadsheet template: *Implementation Plan Template with Timeline and Milestones*

White paper: *5 Steps to Producing a Bullet-Proof Cost Justification.* This can be one of the most powerful and useful sales tools you ever create!

Checklist: *Purchase Requisition Information Checklist.* A private cheat sheet of all the facts and details your customer could possibly need to know about you and your company as they are completing internal paperwork for approval and purchasing. This can be a huge time-saver and significantly accelerate the deal!

We have to remember that most of the people we work with in our customer's organization aren't professional "buyers." Unless they work in the procurement department, taking steps to buy something is just one of the many hats they wear in a day. And in many cases, they are not all that experienced in taking some of these steps because they don't do them all that often. Anything we can offer them to help streamline the process, make it easier, or save them time is a huge win for your customer.

5. Approve and Commit

As your customer works through their approval and purchasing process—the "deal path," as I like to call it—the proposal or requisition often passes through one or more stakeholders that we never have a chance to meet personally. This could be one of the best opportunities to really leverage the true power of asynchronous selling assets. In some instances, our digital assets will be the only exposure some of these stakeholders ever have to us and vice versa. Here are some of the actions that might be involved in the approval and commitment stage:

- Obtain all needed approvals and signatures
- Secure funding of financing for the expenditure
- Check references
- Have contract approved by the legal department
- Process purchase through procurement

These are probably only a few of the steps involved in your customers' approval and purchasing process. As I mentioned earlier, buying processes vary greatly based on a host of different factors. The idea is to try to identify the various steps your customer has to take in each of the seven major stages of the buying cycle and provide whatever digital assets you can to empower and enable them to take each step. Here are a few assets that might apply in the approval and commitment phase:

Checklist: *5 Things You Can Do to Expedite Obtaining Approval Before You Submit Your Requisition*

Private article: *Best Practices for Improving the Chances of Getting Your Project Funded*

Client reference videos: We've already talked about this multiple times. Here is the perfect place to utilize them!

Contract overview video: Shoot a video walking through your proposal and your contract that can travel with the requisition as it goes from one approver to another. This is the next best thing if you never get the chance to walk each person through the proposal personally.

This idea of a walk-through video is especially important if you never had the opportunity to meet with some of the key stakeholders throughout the buying process. If the deal warrants this much effort, shoot one video specifically for the financial approver, another for the contract approver, one for the final approver, and maybe even one for purchasing. This will give you a chance to go over the salient points of the proposal and the contract that are relevant to each persona.

Just in case you are thinking you don't have time, let me ask you this: If you were given six minutes to meet privately with each of these key stakeholders—whom you otherwise would never have access to—where you could walk them through the proposal, would you take the opportunity to do it? Of course you would!

We have to stop thinking about the selling we do using digital assets as something outside of our core job responsibilities. Selling via every possible medium *is* our job! Technology now allows us to get through doors *digitally* that we could never get through before. Take advantage of it!

6. Implement

Once your customer finalizes their purchase, their real work begins. Now they have to actually use whatever they bought to try to produce the results they promised their management team they could achieve if the investment was funded. Here are a few digital assets that might be helpful:

Checklist: *Supplier and Client Responsibilities and Deliverables.* I absolutely love this tool! It's something that I've been using for many years. In fact, I always introduce it in the approve and commit stage once the time is right to start talking about who's going to be doing what once we get all the approvals and signatures needed to move forward. This is a phenomenal way to make sure that your customer knows what they are responsible for doing through the delivery, installation, or integration phases.

Many of the delays in our internal process—that customers sometimes get upset about—are related to them not providing us with all the information, resources, or access to people and systems that *we* need. Creating a checklist of exactly what is needed and when it's needed can really help reduce finger-pointing and avoidable delays during delivery and implementation.

Spreadsheet template: *Implementation Plan Template with Timeline and Milestones.* I listed this one in phase 4 because that's where it is often introduced. Here is where the plan is executed and managed to completion. Some product and services rollouts required elaborate Gantt chart timelines and diagrams to visualize who needs to do what. Others can be defined with a few delivery dates and a payment schedule. But providing the digital tools that allow your client to track progress toward completion is one of the best ways I know to keep everyone accountable and committed to the stated goals and objectives of the project.

7. Assess and Measure

As I mentioned earlier, while we might think of assess and measure as the last stage in the process, it can also be the first stage of the *next* buying process if we work it right. If you've recently completed a project or are still on the way to completion, assessment can be a terrific way to prove that you delivered as promised *and* to reveal the potential opportunity for future partnership. If a prospective client is considering working with you for the first time, assessing and measuring their performance can be a great way to prove yourself and earn the credibility and trust needed to win an opportunity to serve them. Here are a few examples of how digital assets could be used for this:

Video: *9 Things You Have to Know to Assess the Health of Your Business*

Article: *5 Early Indicators of Impending Disaster for* _____ *Manufacturers*

White paper: *Why Smart Companies Should Reassess Their Vendors Every 18 to 24 Months.* (Note: This is a perfect example of an asset you may not want to post publicly or send to your existing clients. You might want to offer it as a link in an email to target accounts that don't currently do business with you. But then again, if you are confident enough in how you stack up against the competition, maybe you would be happy to prove yourself to be the best choice again every year or two.)

Industry benchmarks: The idea of industry benchmarks is very appealing. Companies are always curious to know how they are performing compared to their competitors or to their peers.

If you are able to collect data on various key performance indicators across organizations, and then enable your prospective clients to compare themselves to their contemporaries, that can be a fantastic way to start a relationship.

Many companies charge a fee for these kinds of assessments and the benchmark analysis. Depending on the nature of your business, this kind of data can be challenging to obtain. And, of course, you have to conduct the comparison in a way that doesn't compromise proprietary or privileged information. But you don't have to produce all the empirical data yourself. There are many research analyst organizations that publish benchmark data specific to certain industries. You can offer to help your prospects assess their own performance and compare themselves to industry averages.

* * *

As extensive as this exploration has been, these examples probably represent a mere fraction of customer buying actions required to make an investment in the kinds of complex solutions that many of us sell. I've tried to present all of these ideas as a way to help you save time and continue advancing a buying process even when you can't be present with the customer. This will help you drive time out of your sales cycles! But I want to make one more really important point.

When you help arm your customer with the information and the insight they need to be more efficient and effective throughout each stage of their buying process, you are adding tremendous value. You are differentiating yourself as a real partner who is helping them get from Point A, through Point B, all the way to Point C, and beyond!

These examples of some of the digital assets you can use to facilitate your customer's buying process and close more sales opportunities are barely the tip of the iceberg. The possibilities are literally endless. If you start to proactively look for ways you could help your customers take each step in their buying process, and then digitize as much of that help as possible, you will make yourself an invaluable resource. You'll become a partner they want to come back to over and over. And they'll tell all their friends, too!

Putting These Ideas into Practice

Here are some steps you can take to make the most of what is in this chapter:

1. *Map Out Your Customer's Buying Process*

   Start with a high-level map of a typical buying process for the types of customers you work with, including the buying roles (the people involved) in each stage. This was suggested earlier in this chapter. Keep in mind that if you sell different kinds of products and services to different kinds of customers and perhaps to different industries,

(continued)

one buying process does not fit all. But don't overcomplicate things. Pick one that is relevant for a large percentage of your customers and start there.

2. *Think Like the Buyer*

   Look at each major stage in your customer's buying process and think about the buying steps they have to take. This is a perfect example of learning to "think like a fish." Give some thought to what conclusions they are drawing, the decisions they are making, and the actions they have to take to move the buying process forward within each stage.

3. *Design and Create Your Digital Selling Assets*

   Come up with a least one idea for a digital asset that would help your customer take each step in their process. Ask yourself, "What information or data would help them when taking this step or making this decision?" Or better yet, literally ask your customers! Become interested or maybe even fanatical about helping your customers buy. Learn the steps they have to work through. Then figure out a way to provide the insight and guidance they need every step of the way.

Notes

Introduction

1. Andrea Hsu, "New Businesses Soared to Record Highs in 2021. Here's a Taste of One of Them," NPR, January 12, 2022, https://www.npr.org/2022 /01/12/1072057249/new-business-applications-record-high-great-resignation -pandemic-entrepreneur.
2. Jay McBain, "Through-Channel Marketing Represents the Third Stage for Sales and Marketing Leaders," Forrester, April 25, 2018, https://www.forrester .com/blogs/through-channel-marketing-represents-the-third-stage-for-sales -and-marketing-leaders/.

Chapter 1

1. "The B2B Buying Journey," Gartner, accessed June 7, 2022, https://www .gartner.com/en/sales/insights/b2b-buying-journey.
2. "Distribution of Buying Groups' Time by Key Buying Activities," Gartner, © 2019 Gartner, Inc. and/or its affiliates. All rights reserved. CM_611049. https:// www.gartner.com/en/sales/insights/b2b-buying-journey.
3. Sushant Khandelwal, David Deming, Jens Friis Hjortegaard, and Wade Cruse, "Virtual Selling Has Become Simply Selling," Bain & Company, April 2, 2021, https://www.bain.com/insights/virtual-selling-has-become-simply-selling/.
4. Ayal Steinberg, "98% of Enterprise Purchases Start with a Google Search," Selling with Data, May 1, 2022, https://sellingwithdata.substack.com/p/3-98 -of-enterprise-purchases-start?s=r.
5. Kelly Blum, "Future of Sales 2025: Why B2B Sales Needs a Digital-First Approach," Gartner, September 23, 2020, https://www.gartner.com/smarterwithgartner/future -of-sales-2025-why-b2b-sales-needs-a-digital-first-approach.
6. L. Ceci, "How Much Time on Average Do You Spend on Your Phone on a Daily Basis?," Statista, February 25, 2022, https://www.statista.com/statistics /1224510/time-spent-per-day-on-smartphone-us/.
7. Sheryl Sandberg, quoted in "Inside the Mind of Facebook's Sheryl Sandberg," Blue Sky Partners, *Chicago Tribune*, October 10, 2015, https://www .chicagotribune.com/business/blue-sky/ct-inc-interview-with-sheryl-sandberg -bsi-hub-20151010-story.html.

8. "Organic Search Improves Ability to Map to Consumer Intent," Brightedge Research, 2019, https://videos.brightedge.com/research-report/BrightEdge _ChannelReport2019_FINAL.pdf.
9. "Advertising," *Merriam-Webster.com*, 2022, https://www.merriam-webster .com/dictionary/advertising.

Chapter 2

1. Karl Schmidt, Brent Adamson, and Anna Bird, "Making the Consensus Sale," *Harvard Business Review*, March 2015, https://hbr.org/2015/03/making-the -consensus-sale.
2. Chet Holmes, *The Ultimate Sales Machine* (Penguin Publishing Group, 2007).

Chapter 3

1. "Ninjio Aware Reviews," Gartner, Accessed June 8, 2022, https://www.gartner .com/reviews/market/security-awareness-computer-based-training/vendor /ninjio/product/ninjio-aware.

Chapter 4

1. Dale Lampertz, "Has Cold Calling Gone Cold?," Baylor University's Keller Center for Research, September 2012, https://www.baylor.edu/content/services /document.php/183060.pdf.
2. Andy Gilhooley, "SMS Marketing vs. Email Marketing: Who Wins the Battle for Effectiveness?" RedEye, May 4, 2021, https://www.redeye.com/resources /sms-marketing-vs-email-marketing-who-wins-the-battle-for-effectiveness/ #:~:text=The%20average%20open%20rate%20of,a%20friend%20or %20family%22member.

Chapter 6

1. Bill Stoller, "71% of Hiring Decision-Makers Agree Social Media Is Effective for Screening Applicants," Cision PRWeb, October 14, 2020, https://www .prweb.com/releases/71_of_hiring_decision_makers_agree_social_media_is _effective_for_screening_applicants/prweb17467312.htm.
2. Jordan Grimmer, "Experts vs. Friends: The Definitive Guide to Who Influences Us and Why," The Bottom Line, September 29, 2016, https://medium .com/bestcompany/experts-vs-friends-the-definitive-guide-to-who-influences -us-and-why-6a0aa609c8c0.
3. "Patience" *Lexico.com*, 2022, https://www.lexico.com/en/definition/patience.

Chapter 7

1. Kyle Norton, "Using Personal Video to 3x Response Rates and Boost Sales Performance," Vidyard, Accessed June 9, 2022, https://www.vidyard.com /customers/league-sales-video-success-story/.

Index

Page numbers followed by *f* refers to figures

About the Author

Bill Stinnett is the founder and president of Sales Excellence International and is a highly sought after speaker and trainer appearing at sales meetings, conferences, conventions, and annual sales kick-offs worldwide. He is the author of two previous best-selling books, *Think Like Your Customer* (McGraw Hill 2005) and *Selling Results!* (McGraw Hill 2007) and creator of numerous online sales training programs. His corporate clients include Verizon, Microsoft, IBM, General Electric, Cisco, Hitachi, Harvard Business School and over 400 other companies of every size. For more information, or to request Bill for your next event, please call 1-800-524-1994 or visit www.salesexcellence.com.